Suicide

David M. Haugen and Matthew J. Box,
Book Editors

Bruce Glassman, Vice President
Bonnie Szumski, Publisher
Helen Cothran, Managing Editor
Scott Barbour, Series Editor

GREENHAVEN PRESS

An imprint of Thomson Gale, a part of The Thomson Corporation

THOMSON
＊
™
GALE

Detroit • New York • San Francisco • San Diego • New Haven, Conn.
Waterville, Maine • London • Munich

LIBRARY OF CONGRESS CATALOGING-IN-PUBLICATION DATA

Suicide / David M. Haugen and Matthew J. Box, book editors.
   p. cm. — (Social issues firsthand)
   Includes bibliographical references and index.
   ISBN 0-7377-2905-8 (lib. bdg. : alk. paper)
      1. Suicide. I. Haugen, David M., 1969– . II. Box, Matthew J., 1976– . III. Series.
   HV6545.S8142   2006
   362.28—dc22   2005046239

Printed in the United States of America

CONTENTS

The intended "last words" of suicide victims and those
who have contemplated suicide reveal their failure to
communicate emotions and bespeak their skewed justi-
fications for taking their own lives.

The suicide note of a closeted gay teenager spews
venom at the friend who let his secret be known in
school and at those classmates who subsequently
abused and made fun of him.

A lonely housewife believes her family's problems are
hers alone. Hoping to relieve the burden on her family,
she takes an overdose of sleeping pills.

After hiding her depression behind a veil of happiness
and eventually attempting suicide, a woman is amazed
when people come to her aid and are willing to support
her in her recovery.

for his own problems and to pass this lesson on to his own children.

CHAPTER 3: THERAPISTS' PERSPECTIVES ON SUICIDE

Social issues are often viewed in abstract terms. Pressing challenges such as poverty, homelessness, and addiction are viewed as problems to be defined and solved. Politicians, social scientists, and other experts engage in debates about the extent of the problems, their causes, and how best to remedy them. Often overlooked in these discussions is the human dimension of the issue. Behind every policy debate over poverty, homelessness, and substance abuse, for example, are real people struggling to make ends meet, to survive life on the streets, and to overcome addiction to drugs and alcohol. Their stories are ubiquitous and compelling. They are the stories of everyday people—perhaps your own family members or friends—and yet they rarely influence the debates taking place in state capitols, the national Congress, or the courts.

The disparity between the public debate and private experience of social issues is well illustrated by looking at the topic of poverty. Each year the U.S. Census Bureau establishes a poverty threshold. A household with an income below the threshold is defined as poor, while a household with an income above the threshold is considered able to live on a basic subsistence level. For example, in 2003 a family of two was considered poor if its income was less than $12,015; a family of four was defined as poor if its income was less than $18,810. Based on this system, the bureau estimates that 35.9 million Americans (12.5 percent of the population) lived below the poverty line in 2003, including 12.9 million children below the age of eighteen.

Commentators disagree about what these statistics mean. Social activists insist that the huge number of officially poor Americans translates into human suffering. Even many families that have incomes above the threshold, they maintain, are likely to be struggling to get by. Other commentators insist that the statistics exaggerate the problem of poverty in the United States. Compared to people in developing countries, they point out, most so-called poor families have a high quality of life. As stated by journalist Fidelis Iyebote, "Cars are owned by 70 percent of 'poor' households. . . . Color televisions belong to 97 percent of the 'poor' [and] videocassette recorders belong to nearly 75 percent. . . . Sixty-four percent have microwave ovens, half own a stereo system, and over a quarter possess an automatic dishwasher."

However, this debate over the poverty threshold and what it means is likely irrelevant to a person living in poverty. Simply put, poor people do not need the government to tell them whether they are poor. They can see it in the stack of bills they cannot pay. They are aware of it when they are forced to choose between paying rent or buying food for their children. They become painfully conscious of it when they lose their homes and are forced to live in their cars or on the streets. Indeed, the written stories of poor people define the meaning of poverty more vividly than a government bureaucracy could ever hope to. Narratives composed by the poor describe losing jobs due to injury or mental illness, depict horrific tales of childhood abuse and spousal violence, recount the loss of friends and family members. They evoke the slipping away of social supports and government assistance, the descent into substance abuse and addiction, the harsh realities of life on the streets. These are the perspectives on poverty that are too often omitted from discussions over the extent of the problem and how to solve it.

Greenhaven Press's Social Issues Firsthand series provides a forum for the often-overlooked human perspectives on society's most divisive topics of debate. Each volume focuses on one social issue and presents a collection of ten to sixteen narratives by those who have had personal involvement with the topic. Extra care has been taken to include a diverse range of perspectives. For example, in the volume on adoption, readers will find the stories of birth parents who have given up their children for adoption, adoptive parents, and adoptees themselves. After exposure to these varied points of view, the reader will have a clearer understanding that adoption is an intense, emotional experience full of joyous highs and painful lows for all concerned.

Each book in the series contains several features that enhance its usefulness, including an in-depth introduction, an annotated table of contents, bibliographies for further research, a list of organizations to contact, and a thorough index. These elements—combined with the poignant voices of people touched by tragedy and triumph—make the Social Issues Firsthand series a valuable resource for research on today's topics of political discussion.

According to the American Association of Suicidology (AAS), suicide ranks higher than homicide as a leading cause of death in America. In 2002 nearly thirty-two thousand people chose to kill themselves, an average of one suicide every sixteen minutes. Suicide accounted for 12 percent of deaths among young people aged fifteen to twenty-four, making it the third-leading cause of death among those in that age group. The suicide rate is particularly high among the elderly: While the elderly made up 12.3 percent of the population, they represented 17.5 percent of the nation's suicides. In addition to the large number of successful suicides, the AAS estimates that more than 750,000 suicides were attempted in 2002 and that about 5 million people have attempted suicide at some point during their life. Most alarming, however, is the belief among analysts that suicidal death is underreported and the true statistics may be more frightening.

These statistics suggest that suicide takes an enormous toll on American society. In an attempt to prevent such tragic loss of life and the grief that it inflicts on the victims' loved ones, experts seek to uncover the causes of suicide. Examining the motives behind suicide is difficult because in most cases the person does not provide the reasons for taking his or her own life. Answers, then, must often be compiled from whatever clues can be gleaned in the aftermath of the act. Suicide notes and the testimony of survivors provide useful insights into the inner workings of the suicidal mind, but the causes of suicide necessarily vary from case to case. While no single cause of suicide can be isolated, most medical experts agree that it is often accompanied by intense feelings of depression and low self-worth.

DEPRESSION

Depression is commonly believed to be a factor in most cases of suicide. Depression is a mood disorder that causes symptoms including intense sadness and feelings of failure, guilt, inadequacy, and hopelessness. These feelings are often so overwhelming that they interfere with a person's ability to think rationally about his or her situation. Seeing no way out of the current predicament and no hope for the future, such a person may view suicide as a reasonable way to end his or her suffering. Most experts agree that major depression, the most serious form of the disorder, has a biological cause. Specifically, it is the result of improper levels of certain brain chemicals that control mood. Medication and therapy can help such people by improving their mood and helping them to think more positively about their lives.

In some people, depression may be more episodic. That is, rather than the result of an ongoing chemical imbalance, it may be the result of a life event such as the death of a loved one, the loss of a job, or a divorce. This type of sudden loss can disrupt a person's emotional state. If such a person fails to adjust successfully, he or she can sink into a serious depression, and suicidal behavior may result. Barry Greenwald, a clinical psychologist, writes that,

> loss is experienced as a wound and the individual needs time to heal, to restore his psychic equilibrium. The period following loss is a time of reassessment and revision. Loss requires a new adjustment, a learning to do without whatever has been lost. It is a slow process and often a confusing time as people try to work out how their life is going to be now.[1]

As Greenwald notes, suicidal behavior can potentially come when the period of grief fails to give way to healthy adjustment and a return to emotional balance.

An eroded sense of self-worth may also contribute to depression and suicide. Feeling like a valued member of a community is an innately human need. Rejection by one's peers can result in intense feelings of despair. For example, a 1999 study in Boston revealed that gay teens are more than three times as likely as heterosexual teens to commit suicide. Although no defining motive was uncovered, researchers argued that homophobic persecution and feelings of isolation from their peers were probable contributing factors. Overweight teenagers also commonly suffer such abuse, as do many other teenagers who adhere to some image or behavior outside the mainstream. Existing data, however, fails to either support or deny that there is a clear connection between persecution and suicide. After all, many teens suffer abuse from bullies or remain social outcasts without resorting to suicide. Still, many experts continue to argue that low self-esteem is a gateway to suicidal behavior.

Low self-esteem may also be a factor in copycat suicides—those motivated by the suicidal death of a friend, family member, or influential figure in youth culture such as a celebrated musician or a famed author. Friends, relatives, and pop icons serve as role models to young people, who often endow them with more wisdom and insight than they actually possess. This tendency to exaggerate the wisdom of role models results in part from a young person's lack of strong identity combined with a desire to be taken seriously and to have an assured persona that bespeaks confidence, belonging, and purpose. In an article on copycat suicides for the 2004 issue of *InPsych*, the journal of the Australian Psychological Society, Michael Carr-Gregg, a psychologist specializing in treating adolescents, states that, "many young people . . . don't believe in themselves, they don't have a basic sense of meaning, purpose or belonging."[2] He implies that this lack of self-purpose makes young people more willing to imitate the suicides of others who seemingly have the answers to life's secrets or simply have come to the conclusion that life is not worth living.

Unfortunately, copycat suicides often occur in clusters—especially among young people—and may be promoted by the media attention garnered by the original suicide. Stephen Soreff, president of Education Initiatives in Worcester, Massachusetts, writes, "Suicides by friends provoke others to duplicate the event. Especially in adolescents, suicide has a contagious aspect. Not uncommonly, one suicide in a high school will be followed by other suicides or attempts."[3] These cluster suicides may demonstrate not only young people's desire to follow leaders but also their desire for attention—even if it is achieved posthumously.

Along with depression and a poor self-image, addiction may also contribute to suicide in some cases. According to data compiled by the National Center for Health Statistics, 30 percent of those who had committed suicide in the year 2001 had previously been diagnosed with alcoholism. The cause-and-effect relationship between addiction and suicide is unclear. People who are depressed often turn to drugs and alcohol in an attempt to ease their suffering, so in many cases it may be unclear whether addiction or depression is the truest underlying cause of the suicide. However, many clinicians believe that drugs and alcohol may lower inhibitions and allow suicidal feelings already within a person to have free rein.

Whatever its cause, the act of taking one's own life continues to perplex humanity. To counter the phenomenon, professionals and educators have undertaken serious efforts to increase suicide awareness in society. Publications, Web sites, crisis hotlines, and support groups are ubiquitous on all of the continents of the world, encouraging people to stay alert for symptoms and to offer intervention in times of desperation. However, suicide statistics have fluctuated only minimally in recent years. This trend may indicate that, despite efforts to prevent its occurrence, suicide may remain a mystery and a tragic fact of life.

NOTES

1. Barry Greenwald, "Loneliness, Depression, and Suicide," Convening Web site. www.uic.edu/orgs/convening/depress.htm.
2. Quoted in Steven Gregor, "Copycat Suicide: The Influence of the Media," *InPsych*, August 2004. www.psychology.org.au/publications/in psych/12.2_81.asp.
3. Stephen Soreff, "Suicide," E-Medicine, March 14, 2005. www.emedi cine.com/med/topic3004.htm.

CHAPTER 1

Suicide Notes and Attempts

Famous Suicide Notes

by Virginia Woolf and Hermann Göring

According to Marc Etkind, the author of . . . *Or Not To Be: A Collection of Suicide Notes*, suicide victims only began the now-common practice of leaving suicide notes in the eighteenth century. He contends that the emergence of suicide notes coincided with the rise of the newspaper as a form of communication. The reason for this, Etkind claims, is that suicide notes are an attempt to communicate—to explain one's death, to justify the act, or perhaps to enact some form of emotional revenge.

The following suicide notes were written by two famous individuals. The first was written by Virginia Woolf, a famed British novelist who suffered from manic depression. Having survived three nervous breakdowns, Woolf decided to end her life before experiencing a fourth. On March 28, 1941, she left her suicide note for her husband to find; she then went to a nearby river and drowned herself. Her note lays out her reasons for suicide and blames herself for her depression's effects on her relationship with her husband.

The next three notes in this collection were written by Hermann Göring, the head of Nazi Germany's air force. Göring had been captured at the end of World War II by Allied forces and was sentenced to death by a war crimes tribunal. Not content with being hanged at the hands of his enemies, Göring decided to end his own life by taking a dose of cyanide that he supposedly had secreted on his person. Before taking the poison on October 15, 1946, Göring wrote out three notes in the privacy of his cell. One was addressed to the Allied Control Council that had condemned him for his crimes; another was destined for his pastor; the third was addressed to his wife.

WOOLF'S NOTE

Dearest,
 I feel certain I am going mad again. I feel we can't go through another of those terrible times. And I shan't recover this

Part I: Quentin Bell, *Biography: Virginia Woolf*. Orlando, FL: Harcourt Brace & Company, 1972. Copyright © 1972 by Quentin Bell. All rights reserved. Reproduced by permission of the publisher. Part II: David Irving, *Göring: A Biography*. New York: Morrow, 1989. Copyright © 1989 by Morrow. Reproduced by permission of the author.

time. I begin to hear voices, and I can't concentrate. So I am doing what seems the best thing to do. You have been in every way all that anyone could be. I don't think two people could have been happier till this terrible disease came. I can't fight any longer. I know that I am spoiling your life, that without me you could work. And I know you will. You see I can't even write this properly. I can't read. What I want to say is I owe all the happiness of my life to you. You have been entirely patient with me and incredibly good. I want to say that—everybody knows it. If anybody could have saved me it would have been you. Everything has gone from me but the certainty of your goodness. I can't go on spoiling your life any longer.

I don't think two people could have been happier than we have been.

GÖRING'S NOTES

To the Allied Control Council:

I would have let you shoot me without further ado! But it is not possible to hang the German Reichsmarschall! I cannot permit this, for Germany's sake. Besides, I have no moral obligation to submit to the justice of my enemies. I have therefore chosen the manner of death of the great Hannibal.

It was clear from the outset that a death sentence would be pronounced against me, as I have always regarded the trial as a purely political act by the victors, but I wanted to see this trial through for my people's sake and I did at least expect that I should not be denied a soldier's death. Before God, my country, and my conscience I feel myself free of the blame that an enemy tribunal has attached to me.

Dear Pastor Gerecke!

Forgive me, but I had to do it like this for political reasons. I have prayed long to my God and feel that I am doing the right thing. (I would have let them shoot me.) Please comfort my wife and tell her that this was no ordinary suicide, and that she can rest assured that God will still gather me up in His great mercy!

God protect my dearest ones!

God bless you, dear pastor, evermore.

Your Hermann Göring.

My only sweetheart!

Upon mature consideration and after profound prayers to my God, I have decided to take my own life and thus not allow my enemies to execute me. I would always have accepted death by firing squad. But the Reichsmarschall of Greater Germany can not allow himself to be hanged. Moreover, the killings were to be carried out like a spectacle with the press and film cameras there (I assume for the newsreel pictures). Sensation is all that matters.

I however want to die quietly and out of the public eye. My life came to an end the moment I said my last farewell to you. Since then I am filled with a wondrous peace and I regard death as the final release.

I take it as a sign from God that throughout the months of my imprisonment He allowed me the means to free myself from this mortal coil, and that this means was never discovered. In His charity, God thus spared me the bitter end.

All my thoughts are with you, with Edda, and all my beloved friends! The last beats of my heart will mark our great and eternal love.

Your Hermann

The Suicide Note of a Gay Teen

by Steven

While those who have had the time to plan their own deaths may leave behind thoughtful, pensive suicide notes, some suicide victims scribble out their last words in haste before committing the rash act. The following narrative is an excerpt from the suicide note of a young man named Steven. At the time the note was written, Steven was sixteen years old and struggling with being a homosexual. According to Steven, he confided his sexuality to a friend he thought he could trust, only to find that she told his secret to many people. As a result, he had become the victim of ceaseless taunting and bullying. His note declares that the negative reactions of his peers have made his life unbearable and that the only way he can escape the pain is by killing himself.

After writing the note, Steven attempted to commit suicide by taking an overdose of medication. He has since recovered, and he and his family have moved to another state.

I am sorry to the people that I love but I can't f##king take it anymore. So I am gay. Why does everyone hate me because of that? F##k them. I have been punched and spit on and called faggot, queer, loser, pussy, fag boy. Some asshole painted faggot on my locker. Some people do not talk to me. F##k them, f##k everyone, I hate this f##king life now. I am so f##king tired of the s##t. I have received hate letters telling me to leave school, telling me that faggots aren't welcome and that I am a fag.

I am scared and I am tired and I can't take any more. Yesterday in the locker room some assholes said Steven is such a pussy and faggot. He is an ugly stupid faggot and we should kill him. And they knew that I could hear them. I don't know what to f##king think now. Is it better that they kill me or I kill myself, I don't f##king know. I just want to die and that is all so I don't have to put up with this f##king s##t. . . . I hate everyone now. I am a better person than any one of them and I f##king know that for sure. I don't want to be such a f##king problem for my family either. After all, you have a fag for a son. Why do people need to do this and we did nothing. They should all be in prison. They are horrible. I hate every f##king one, so f##k them.

I HAVE TO DIE

I know this that they are assholes. I wish that they could feel this s##t that I feel then see what they do. They could not f##king take it and I know that without a doubt. So why is this life so f##ked? Why? I just am going to end everything now. This is it. I need to kill myself. I love many people. Mom and Dad, I love you and you didn't do anything bad. I hate life and this is why I have to die. I am scared and I am tired of being laughed at, made fun of, beaten up, and threatened and s##t and feeling like s##t. . . . I just need to die. Don't be mad. Be happy that all the bad s##t I feel is going to be over finally forever. God will understand, and I know that. Maybe Jesus was gay. How do we know anything? Maybe god is gay. I am gay and I should not be f##ked over because of that. So f##king what. People are just too stupid. I am like every f##king other person, just I am gay. So f##king what. Assholes. I should paint asshole on everyone's locker before I die. I just don't care anymore. I need to go. I am so scared now. I know I need to die, but I will be fine after I am dead. I am so sure of that because god will take care of me. I never did anything wrong and I know I will go to heaven. And I hope the assholes go to hell. . . .

I have thought for a long time about committing suicide. I need to kill myself. No other asshole is going to kill me. I will commit suicide, and I will have peace and be freed. So I need to do this. You must understand. I can not live one more day. I will be so happy in heaven. I can just be normal like everyone else. I will not be the faggot, the queer, the fag boy, the pussy.

I have wanted to be dead for so long. I don't really know how I made it as far as this because I just think about being dead. I am never happy. Why did so many people lie to me? I wish I never told anyone I am gay. Why the fuck did I do that? [Name removed] started this. I wish she was dead. I trusted her. . . . So I tell [name removed] because I was so f##king tired of hiding everyday. F##k her, the bitch. I hate her. She killed me.

LIKE BEING IN HELL

I love you Mom and Dad because, even though you did not understand, maybe you loved me and said I was fine and you would help me. But at school it was like being in hell. I was burning in hell every day. I could not tell you everything that was happening. I did not want you to worry about me. I could not do that to you. I hope that you will forgive me. Please forgive me. And remember me when I was happy. And I am not a faggot. I am a person that is all. Why was I a gay though, why me, why, why, why, why I always ask. I will never know. God must have wanted me to be with him now because he is telling me to kill myself. . . . Don't be sad. You won't have a faggot son anymore. So you will be happy. No more burden for you. Tell everyone I got sick, or something. It doesn't matter. I just can't go on one day more. I cannot f##king go on. . . . I love you Mom and Dad, and I do have some friends and not many. But, most everyone is a stupid asshole and I hope that they get sick and die. I hate them for what they did and most of all [name removed] because she started it all. I hate her. . . .

I know that life is horrible now. It is not worth living. It really is not worth living. Why should I go on? You must understand me. I can't go through this any more. I am scared everyday. I feel like s##t everyday. I don't want to go out anymore. I never want to go to school. How can I learn anything? I can't. I don't care. Grades, so what? And then I will work and people will call me fag. I will always be a fag to them. . . .

No, I won't let anyone else hurt me. That is another reason why I will commit suicide. Nobody will hurt me again, ever, ever. No one will call me a fag or a queer or a pussy or a fag boy or anything. Nobody is going to spit on me again. Or write faggot on my locker or send me letters telling me that I should go to another school because I am a faggot, or say they should kill me because I am an ugly faggot. . . .

[Name removed] started this s##t, and she should be imprisoned forever. Now I can't stop crying. I am so f##ked up, my head is so f##ked up. Mom and Dad, I am sorry. I need to die. Just understand. Please understand and never stop loving me. It is not your [fault]. And don't be sad, please, never be sad. I feel so sick, but I kind of feel happy, too, because I know it will be over soon. I don't know about what everything will be like. I am kind of scared too. But I have to die now because I can not take one more day. I can not take one more f##king day of them saying fag, queer, hitting me, spitting at me. They spit on me. Goddamn assholes. . . .

Why did all of this happen? My head is just so f##ked up. I am sad always. I don't remember when I was happy. It was so long ago, or was I ever happy? Can faggots be happy? I don't know, but I am not a faggot. They are faggots, and I am a person. I feel so much pain all of the time. I guess you could say that I am like numb. Because I am. Just pain, all pain. And I hate the pain. It is like they beat the hell out of me with their stupid words. I guess that they do. They don't win. I will win because I will be happy and they are horrible people. F##k, I can't stop crying, but I am very happy too. It is weird. I guess I am crying because I am sorry, Mom and Dad. But, I am happy that I will be in heaven and no more attacks. . . .

I WILL BE HAPPY

What is heaven really like, Mom and Dad? I hope it is all that's not here. And don't be sad because you will be with me again. I know. I know.

I am getting happier now. I am because it is all ending now. I want you to know that I feel good now. I think I feel really good now, yes I do. I am not crying anymore, and I am feeling happy. I think I will be happy in heaven—no longer a faggot just a person. . . .

I have to say goodbye now, so don't be sad. Please never be sad. I am happy. I am really happy now. Everything will be fine. I am happier than I have ever been because it is all over.

Goodbye, I love you, Mom and Dad, but I hate almost everyone else. Don't be sad.

I am happy now.

Attempting to Rid My Family of My Toxic Presence

by Chris, with Richard A. Heckler

In his book *Waking Up Alive*, Richard A. Heckler attempts to elucidate the experiences of people taken to the brink of suicide. In the following excerpt, Heckler helps to relate the story of the attempted suicide of a woman named Chris. Chris tells of the helplessness and exasperation that drove her to contemplate and attempt suicide, and her words are augmented by Heckler's perceptions of her story.

Chris provides a graphic account of her life: a miserable and unfulfilling marriage, severe loneliness, and the inability to find sympathy from those around her. Already plagued by these troubles, Chris then suffers an unexpected pregnancy and a violent argument with her husband. As Heckler explains, these two "precipitating events" finally trigger a loss of rationality, ultimately driving her to finally attempt suicide by overdosing on sleeping pills. Chris maintains that her confused state made her believe that her troubles and her family's ills were caused by her "poisonous" presence. Only after being taken into a therapeutic environment does Chris come back to reality, and she is left feeling embarrassed that people had to see her in such a disastrous state of mind.

Richard A. Heckler is the director of the Hakomi Institute of San Francisco and is a trainer of therapists throughout the United States. He is also an associate professor of counseling at JFK University in California and a teacher at the Union Institute of Experimental Studies in Ohio.

When I got married, I had this whole picture: the good wife and mother, the good daughter, the whole American pie-in-the-sky picture. I just worked so hard at it: to read all the

Richard A. Heckler, *Waking Up Alive: The Descent, the Suicide Attempt, and the Return to Life*. New York: G.P. Putnam's Sons, 1994. Copyright © 1994 by Richard A. Heckler, PhD. Reproduced by permission of Loretta Barrett Books, Inc.

child-care manuals, to be the perfect supermom, to make sure the house was spotless, to do everything for my husband. And then the whole picture died. I did all the stuff other military wives did, but I was blamed when he wasn't promoted. I just wasn't a good navy officer's wife. . . .

Chris is a large woman, big-boned and a little heavy. Her arms were muscular, her hands veined and rough-hewn. This is a woman who has lived in the country, worked the land, canned her own food in the summer, found a way to make things work in difficult times. She is not afraid to be physical. She isn't averse to hard work. She has a ready smile and a hearty laugh, and when she speaks about her life, she is straightforward and candid, eschewing both drama and false modesty. Chris's story vividly illustrates her paradoxical determination to wrest control of her life, by means of her death. It also reflects once again how traumatic loss, unacknowledged, may form the seeds of suicide.

A TOUGH MARRIAGE

As a young woman, Chris found herself foundering in a marriage that was painful and disempowering. She was targeted as the problem—the cause of all the family's misfortune—and after many years, she had come to believe it too.

He was an officer stationed in Oahu [Hawaii] during the war. We got married, he went to boot camp, and he came out thinking, "What the hell am I doing married?"; but he didn't have the courage to just say, "We need to end this," and neither did I. So I hung out for the next eight years with him not wanting me and me trying really hard to be "good enough." I don't think he hated me; it was just all of a sudden he had this whole other life, the navy, thrown at him and he didn't know how to handle it. I became extremely sensitive to criticism— overly sensitive, you know. If anyone criticized me, I felt like I didn't deserve to live. He spent most of his time at the barracks, not coming home for long periods, so it was just me and our daughter, and he didn't care much about her because she was a girl. I got real depressed. It felt like this heavy weight descended on me. I felt lonely—scared—and was growing very tired.

Chris and her husband moved back to the mainland, bought an

old farmhouse, and tried to make a new start, but nothing changed. He continued to distance himself and assign blame, and she grew morose and pained. The grief of his rejection was omnipresent and consuming. For months on end, they would barely speak, occasionally being sexual—for him a release, and for her a momentary respite from loneliness. Curiously, Chris seemed incapable of expressing anger, as though those feelings were being consistently short-circuited, undermined by sadness. She had no experience at being assertive. Demanding basic civility seemed inconceivable, and her self-confidence eroded.

I would get this sinking feeling, like the bottom would drop out of my heart, and these thoughts and feelings that "I don't deserve to live" if I got angry at anybody. They could get angry at me, and I didn't like it much, but I certainly couldn't reciprocate. . . .

PRECIPITATING EVENTS

Two events catapulted Chris into her attempt. The first involved loss. She had been sick for three weeks—unusual for her, for she rarely fell ill with colds or the flu. To her horror, Chris discovered she was pregnant. She needed counsel, but talking about it with her husband went predictably bad.

I had a lot of turmoil about being an okay mother—not being abusive, 'cause that's how I grew up. I mean, I never abused our daughter, but the temptation was always there. I was doing all right with one child, but I knew inside that with another, I'd lose it. And I knew I wasn't gonna get help from my husband.

So I said, "I really need to tell you that I just found out I'm pregnant." At first he just yelled, "I'm not ever living with you again!" When he stopped yelling at me, I told him I thought we should have an abortion and then he just casually said, "Oh well, that's probably a good idea. We couldn't afford a baby right now anyway." He didn't ask me how I was feeling at all! Some time went by and it suddenly occurred to him that he was fertile. He yelled, "Whoa! I got you pregnant!" and he became excited because he had always had a low sperm count and it bothered him a lot. So all of a sudden, he's on this ego trip, while my life is falling apart. I didn't even tell him what I was feeling. I just went ahead.

Chris numbed herself and had the abortion. She had calculated her options as best as she could. She felt that if they had the child, she might never pull free from her husband, and she realized that her situation would only worsen. She could not imagine bringing another child into her broken family, and she no longer believed that she could maintain the composure it would require. The weeks following were some of her most difficult. She wept unceasingly and her isolation felt insurmountable.

I couldn't stop crying. I couldn't regain the control I had, and after a while I couldn't even get a handle on what I was crying about. Every night, I sat on the couch crying. It felt like I even lost track of who was sad. It didn't make a difference anymore. It felt like all there was in the world was sadness. It permeated everything. I started feeling possessed by the house and possessed by the mood, so I would take walks in the woods and on the mountains with my daughter. She was three and a half. We'd spend the day in the fields, or by the river that ran through town, and I'd feel better. And then I'd come home and it would all descend on me again. I even made two trips to a town seventy miles away to see about moving, but all I could do was cry when I got there. I felt wrong for wanting to leave.

It was like a trap set on the floor of the forest, invisible and ready to ensnare the unsuspecting. Every effort Chris made toward self-preservation, deciding to assert herself and leave her suffocating predicament, would trigger waves of doubt and engulf her in self-recrimination.

I'd ask, "What if it's just because I'm in a low mood?" Or I'd say to myself, "It's all my fault. I'm ruining my family's life. I'm breaking up my home. I'm just like my mother."

Chris could not envision a change. She could identify no one close enough, nothing powerful enough, to alter the downward course of her life. One night, after hurling invectives at one another, she and her husband began to hurl the furniture. A huge fight ensued. To Chris's astonishment, she heaved a Volkswagen clutch housing directly at her husband's head. He ducked just in time, and it crashed through the glass front door. They both stood frozen for a moment, shards of the pane diffracting the light from the porch, and then quietly, without another word, she turned and slowly mounted the stairs to the bedroom.

A TOXIC PRESENCE

The pain was up here in my heart, but in the pit of my stom- ach it felt like everything just dropped out of me, out the bot- tom. There was just horror. I had these two bottles of sleeping pills; the doctor kept prescribing them, and I kept on not tak- ing them, just saving them. I knew that would be enough. As I was walking upstairs, I felt cold all through my body, but also determined. It felt like it was the only reasonable thing to do.

This was the second trigger. Chris had finally become angry, but she felt her rage to be poisonous. The fight and her interpretation of it only pushed her further into the tunnel and hurtled her toward her attempt. As she walked upstairs, she thought how much better it would be for her child with her mother dead. She would be reliev- ing everyone of her toxic presence.

I was having thoughts like, "It will be better for my daughter. Her father can raise her. She needs not to be poisoned by me." I remembered that after my father died, his mother—my grandmother—came over in a rage one day and screamed at my mother that if it weren't for her and the kids, my father would be alive. Somehow, I was really bad for people.

A number of disparate feelings swirled within her at the same time. She felt a coldness within her. It penetrated her muscles and bones and she felt it in her heart, as if she were freezing. She also felt herself calmly determined. She wouldn't be deterred, and there was no need to be demonstrative. She would simply take the sleep- ing pills she had saved, fall asleep and not wake up. . . .

Chris methodically swallowed two bottles of sleeping pills and went to bed. She lay there looking out the window, with a feeling of acceptance.

It was like the Last Supper. I was lying in bed, thinking, "These are my last memories." I was savoring them. I wasn't feeling scared. I just felt peaceful and cold.

UNEXPECTED INTERVENTION

It was not clear how much time passed, but suddenly Chris noticed a presence in the room. Her daughter was standing by the bed. She had awakened and come upstairs—something which had never happened before—and she was looking at the bottles. She seemed to understand, and became frightened. In an instant, she grabbed the bottles and ran downstairs to her father. A dramatic chase ensued—a desperate series of events in which Chris fought to die.

> *I was thinking, "Oh, shit! This is not what I planned." I overheard my husband calling an ambulance. The nearest hospital was twenty-five miles away, with winding roads, so I got up and dressed as quickly as I could. I was getting pretty drowsy, but I ran downstairs to go out the door. He grabbed me there, but I got loose from him. I was thinking, "You're not gonna stop me!" and I started running down the street. It's about one A.M. in this little town of sixty people and my daughter came out screaming at me, "Mommy, don't go! Mommy, don't leave me!" It just tore up my heart, but I couldn't change my mind at that point. I was just unable to be rational anymore, and I still thought it was the best thing to do for her.*

Each obstacle reinforced Chris's determination. She knew the small town well, and ran to a spot hidden beneath a bridge down by the river. It had been her secret hiding place, where she knew she would not be found. She lay down, and discovered herself beginning to calm once again. Her legs felt rubbery and a drowsiness began descending upon her.

> *I was losing muscular control and it was getting harder to move, so I just lay there, and I realized I'm back in this beautiful scenery—the river, the full moon. I wasn't going to let go of that. I absolutely had to have that as I drifted away.*

Once again, though, her fragile tranquility was shattered. In the distance, she heard a noise. It seemed out of place so late at night, in such a sleepy little town. She barely noticed it at first, but it grew in pitch and volume. She sensed it had to do with her.

> *I heard bloodhounds! My husband ran to a neighbor with a piece of my clothing, and suddenly I'm being chased by these*

stupid dogs. When they were about half a block from me, I pulled myself up and headed for the center of the bridge. I remember thinking, "Well they're not gonna let me do it my own way, so I'll just jump." I was really determined. I didn't doubt it. I just didn't want to live anymore.

ASSERTING HER SELF-DETERMINATION

Chris felt a mix of panic and anger. She was alarmed that her husband would thwart her plans, and angry that her autonomy was being compromised. For Chris was not simply fighting to die. In the tunnel, in this highly exaggerated state, her wish to kill herself represented a number of conflicting desires, all highly compressed and highly charged. First, suicide served as an exit from the pain with which she had labored so long. Second, as if she were executing a death sentence from somewhere or someone else, her wish to die reflected a deep self-loathing. She actually believed that everyone would be better off after she died. Finally, and perhaps most paradoxically, she was also struggling to assert her right of self-determination. The wish to kill herself represented a desire to manage her life as she chose, as she wished, in whatever form, even death. Self-determination was a critical experience that had eluded her all her life, and she wished for it now.

> *Inside I was screaming, "Why can't I just do what I want to do for once in my life!" I felt, you know, all of these years that he didn't give a shit what was happening to me and now that I've decided this, why the hell does he care! When I really needed him, he wasn't there, and now that I don't, there he is with a half a dozen men and these dogs! Why is he doing this to me?*

Even as her body was beginning to falter, her mind methodically clicked through contingency plans for her suicide. Feeling the press of the chase, she ran to the center of the bridge and climbed onto the railing.

> *I felt this incredible determination, you know, like, "No one can stop me." It was a tremendous sense of power. I jumped from the railing, but as I was in the air, they grabbed me by the ankles. I was hanging upside down, swinging my arms and trying to get free. I was furious! Then they pulled me back onto the bridge. I've never felt so enraged in my life. I*

was fighting them and then I was biting them. They all had their hands on me and were holding me down and I was kicking and screaming. I really hated them at that point. There was no way I wanted to go with them. Somebody took his jacket off, and wrapped me up in it and they just held me down till the ambulance came.

Even in the ambulance, Chris had thoughts of bolting when no one was looking. In this state, she would try whatever it would take to complete the attempt. But she was strapped in, and shortly thereafter the sleeping pills took hold.

Everything just went kind of fuzzy and blank. I got really dizzy and tired and then I kind of collapsed and fell asleep. I was going in and out when I felt them begin to slap me. God, it was a miserable ride. It seemed unreal, feeling so angry and sleepy and being hit repeatedly. At some point I remember beginning to feel horribly embarrased, really ashamed of myself that people were seeing this.

For most, the first moments in the hospital are chilling. There is inevitably a frenzy of activity, focused on either resuscitating the body or sedating the mind. Doctors, nurses, crisis workers, and aides are often quickly on the scene, compounding the confusion as much as helping. Chris's experience was no different, and she would have to survive one hellish night and days of humiliation before beginning to take the steps necessary to extricate herself from her web of hopelessness.

Surviving a Long Battle with Suicidal Depression

by Lena

In the following narrative, a ballet dancer identifying herself as
Lena provides a look inside her suicidal mind. Lena explains that
she suffered from depression for seven years and that she coped
with her problem by hiding behind a facade of happiness. She
states, however, that pretending everything was all right actually
complicated her situation. Claiming that she did not want to
bother others with her emotional instability, Lena denied the
benefits of therapy and sank even further into depression.

Lena's troubles led her to attempt suicide numerous times,
and she admits that her failures to do so worsened her mental
state. Her narrative concludes with an explanation of her most
recent attempt and failure—an attempt in which her family finally discovered her situation and intervened. At the time of her
writing, Lena had reached an eleven-week stint of stability and
had promised her family and her therapist to try to refrain from
acting on her suicidal impulses. She was astounded at the readi-
ness of those around her to come to her aid. She offers a message of hope to others who are struggling with life, asking that
they allow themselves to be open to the possibility of outside
help.

First I will start by telling you who I am, or who everyone else
thinks I am. My name is Lena and I have an identical twin sister.
I am a dancer (ballet that is) and I have been depressed consider-
ably for 7 years. I succeeded in keeping my feelings inside for so
long, no one had a clue.

This is what I was used to though; act happy, be happy, look
happy and everything will be alright. And being miserable seemed to
be my purpose in life. I had to hide these feelings because I didn't
believe anyone else should have to deal with them, or that they
would want to, so I stayed isolated, alone in my head. Only my hell

grew every day and I could no longer hide behind the smiles and the pain, things started falling apart and I couldn't control it anymore.

I started attempting to kill myself, only failing so miserably that I could hide it and never tell another soul. I can't remember exactly what I did or how many times I tried. But I do remember I tried to slit my wrists, which after realizing it was a very difficult thing to do, I started cutting, burning and hitting myself. This only further isolated me in my crazy world. I tried numerous times to overdose with prescriptions and other stuff, but could sleep it off or the effects were not that drastic. I would occasionally try to confide in a friend which only made things worse in my head. I hated for anyone to know the hell I was experiencing so I would always feel extreme guilt and hate myself even more.

THE VEIL OF HAPPINESS

Once in a blue moon I would be able to smile and think things were finally over and I would be ok, but that would only lead to a deeper, darker place in my soul. For each time I dropped down farther and farther into the depths of hell created by me and meant for me. No one would notice and I felt safe hidden behind the happiness, because if I thought everyone perceived me as happy I could ease the pain a little.

The misery grew and I was isolated, letting no one in and letting nothing out. I was more and more depressed every year. High school got worse because I hated the people, could not talk to anyone nor did I want to. A teacher would occasionally express concern and I would plaster my smile on and leave it there for weeks to come until I was convinved they were not worried anymore. A classmate would comment that I resembled a zombie, but still I felt alone and could not feel better. My grades did not drop, my weight stayed the same, I could not leave a trail for someone to find. No normal symptoms would be shown. I was a con artist in my own head.

My doctor would start expressing concern and suggest I see someone, how could I agree, of course I said no. He continually noticed I was depressed and tried to help. But I only shut down more when he would question my suicidal thoughts for I was ashamed of everything I locked in my mind. In my senior year I kept repeatedly trying to overdose and no one was ever the wiser until a friend kept pushing. Then one day an adult found out and I was immediately sent to a therapist. Still feeling extremely depressed I dreamed of dying but felt betrayed and told no one. I graduated in the top of my class, got accepted as an apprentice in a ballet company. My dreams were coming true but I only became more withdrawn and miserable.

I left for the summer program in which I received a scholarship and hoped to find happiness once again. I was wrong; I spiraled farther down. Communicating with a friend long distance I tried to hang on for her I guess. But my dream was dying and I went home, after realizing that to stay would send me deeper inside my hell. And I was in the perfect place to kill myself and knew I would keep trying. So I returned home, where I had been so miserable before. For one more year I would try to fix my life and figure out my pain alone. I was dancing with a professional company and on scholarship, everything I had ever dreamed of. But I still dreamed of dying and could not figure out why.

WAKING UP ALIVE

During my second year out of school I realized I needed a little help in trying to get out of the hell I created by myself. I went to a therapist and then to a psychiatrist for antidepressants. Hoping this would work I tried to open up but I could let nothing out; I was trapped inside my head.

After a normal appointment with my therapist I went home and later to class, having a great class which was very unusual. Later I realized I was unconsiously planning to die. I went home and was very distant and I decided to try to end my life again. It did not strike me as odd that everything I needed was already in place. So I got a glass of water and swallowed 50 pills. Later to realize they were safe drugs unable to end my life. I did not find my eternal sleep; I could not sleep all night. I had no depth perception and I felt like I was lead and could hardly move a finger. I layed in bed all night for about 12 hours. I suffered in silence hoping to die. Later my sister came in asking what was wrong; I never sleep in and it was 11 A.M.! She also knew that I was depressed, and she asked if I had taken too many drugs, being sarcastic, she had no clue. I said yes and the hell began. I never dreamed of WAKING UP ALIVE.

A PROMISE TO HOLD IT TOGETHER

She called my therapist who asked to speak to me and she told me what would happen. My sister called my mom and they took me to the ER [emergency room of a hospital]. I had to drink charcoal and get an IV. I was miserable. Ashamed and degraded I felt bad for causing so much trouble. I tried to tell my mother I was sorry. I really didn't mean to make her feel bad, or live to see it either. She could only question what was so bad? How could I tell her anything but life. After countless hours of observation I was released to wait for an assessment counselor to decide where I would go that night. I refused a psychiatric institute with a women's center but I did not know they could force me; I was horrified but my mind was in control. I told the counselor I would not try again simply because the day had been so terrible. And when I was asked to speak to my therapist she asked me if I felt like I could go home and be safe. I said yes. Needing a reason to believe me, having told her the same thing less than 24 hours before, I gave her my word. I could think of nothing else to say and to my shock she said ok. They conferred longer to see if that was possible and in the end I went home with a few hotline numbers and promises that I would call someone if I planned to hurt myself.

It has been 11 weeks today since that awful emergency room experience. I had to see my therapist twice a week for awhile and my meds were switched. Since then I have been threatened with hospital assessments for expressing my thoughts of death. But I remain in therapy and on medication. Maybe I will feel my cage unlock one day soon so that I can talk about the hell inside. Until then I just exist in this world telling people what they want to hear. I know that can't last forever, that is how I ended up in this place I am in now. But knowing I am still alive after 11 weeks with no improvement, maybe I am stronger than I thought.

So I guess I would like to say that it is not worth all the pain and misery when eventually you will receive help whether or not you want it. So it is much easier to reach out and tell someone you cannot do this alone; it's not worth it. The pain will grow and grow, and so many people are there to help. I could not believe anyone would want to help me but they sure did offer after they found out about my attempt to end my life. Don't let it go that far if you don't have to. Let someone show you the light at the end of their tunnel so maybe you can find your own.

Counseling Helped Me Overcome My Suicidal Feelings

by Elaine G., with Rita Robinson

Rita Robinson is a former health and psychology reporter. She now writes regularly as a freelance author for such publications as *Reader's Digest*, *Cosmopolitan*, and *Men's Fitness*. In her book *Survivors of Suicide*, Robinson recorded the stories of many people who have either attempted suicide or lost a loved one to suicide. One of the people she contacted was Elaine G., a twenty-five-year-old resident of Las Vegas, Nevada. In the following selection from Robinson's book, Elaine tells of how she attempted suicide at age eighteen because of her troubled life and her "past memories that [she] hadn't dealt with." She went into counseling afterward, but, as she states, she did not get the help she needed and eventually quit. Two years later, she voluntarily returned to counseling with the aim of making her life better. As Elaine relates, her new counseling sessions coupled with her determination to live helped her get over her suicidal feelings.

Elaine G. of Las Vegas was 18 when she attempted suicide. At 25, she spoke out about it. She had many of the danger signs and was in counseling at the time. In retrospect she said:

"I didn't really want to die. I just wanted to end the pain. I was in counseling for quite a while before the suicide attempt. I was really messed up. I guess I was looking for somebody to scream out to help me, but it wasn't working. I didn't think anybody understood and it wasn't getting through. I was no longer just thinking about it. It was something I wanted to do. I don't know where the idea for the suicide came from. It was just there. It just came. It was as strong as the urge to live must be. It seemed just another instinct. I thought about it for so long and finally, I no longer thought about it. I said,

'This is what I'm going to do. I'm not happy. I don't want to live. You know you're not going to get run over and die, so you just have to go out and do it yourself.'"

Her stay in the hospital after the attempt changed her thinking. "It shook me. I realized a lot when I was in there. I still had the same feelings. They didn't go away. But I didn't like being locked up in that place. I missed little things—to come and go and to sit outside and talk to friends. I asked myself, 'Do I really want to lose all this?'"

Her counselor was "shook up" about the attempt and told Elaine that she (the counselor) had lost her objectivity. "She told me she was too close to the situation."

THE IMPORTANCE OF AN OBJECTIVE LISTENER

The two are still friends, and Elaine frequents the same counseling center, but sees a different therapist. Elaine believes this is why parents and close friends can only listen and guide you to professional help when a person begins talking about suicide. "You have to talk to someone who can be objective and not give opinions of how wrong it would be of you to commit suicide. Statements such as, 'But you have so much to live for,' or 'Why would someone like you want to commit suicide?' have no meaning to the person who is engulfed in suicidal thought."

She was 20 when she went back into counseling. "For a while I just sort of existed—went with the flow. My life didn't get better, and I had to see if I could make it better. Things started coming around. My perception changed. I just started enjoying life again. I was still doing drugs, but I was older, out of school, and I wasn't suffering from the pressure of school." Although Elaine was still taking drugs, she was able to look back on the suicide attempt and say, "How could I have done that? Life is a growing process and every day I began to appreciate life a little more. It took time to work through and let things change."

Elaine was finally able to give up drugs, although she said it's a continuing battle, and she occasionally slips back into counseling for needed support.

"Drugs didn't make me attempt suicide. The life and the past memories that I hadn't dealt with helped cause the suicide attempt."

Elaine's statement is supported by health professionals who say that drugs and alcohol don't cause suicide. They simply lower the inhibitions about going ahead with plans to end a life. Using drugs and alcohol is just another way of trying to deal with the pain and hurt of what's going on in a person's life.

"Most people who do drugs do it for a reason. They're trying to cover up something or get a feeling they can't get anywhere else. They don't do drugs just for the heck of it, and they don't do drugs just because the other kids are doing it. Until I got counseling I didn't realize there were more serious reasons. And some of those same reasons led to the suicide attempt. It's not one thing. It's a hundred things that build on you and make you do it. You've got to just hang in there and get help. If it takes going to 20 people before you find somebody that makes you comfortable—a qualified professional—then it's worth it," she said.

GUIDING OTHERS TO HELP

Elaine believes it's okay to reach out to parents and friends, but that's only a beginning. By the time a person is contemplating suicide, he or she needs professional help. Parents and friends can listen, and then encourage the person to get in touch with a professional.

"If I hear someone say, 'I wish I was dead,' I don't take that as a light remark. And I don't beat around the bush. I just ask them if they're contemplating suicide. If the person thinks someone cares about their problem, it helps. Just listen to them. Tell them you love them and what to do to get help."

She acknowledges that some people think they don't have the money to pay for counseling. "But the fact is," she says, "there is help for everyone." Most states have programs that assist in counseling fees, and some states are working to see that insurance companies offer some type of payment to cover therapy.

CHAPTER 2

Suicide Survivors' Stories

Dealing with a Lesbian Lover's Suicide

by Catherine

In the following narrative, a woman named Catherine tells of the loss of her lesbian lover, Marion, to suicide in 1988. Catherine explains that Marion had been diagnosed with depression prior to their relationship, but Catherine was not aware of the extent of her lover's illness. Marion's depression, combined with other health problems, Catherine suggests, led to Marion's inability to maintain a will to live.

Catherine's story reveals her efforts to help Marion address her problems, but it also shows her ultimate inability to control Marion's destiny. Catherine also reflects on how some of the couple's mutual friends were fearful of the causes of Marion's death and drifted away after her suicide was disclosed. However, the "white-knuckle ride" that followed Marion's suicide eventually gave way to a stronger bond among Catherine and Marion's two sons from a previous marriage. They were able to move on with their lives without being ashamed of the desperate act of their loved one.

I guess my experience after Marion's death was very similar in some ways to what a married person goes through. All of a sudden, I was isolated. The world travels in couples, and I didn't have the other part of what I needed to function in the groups of people we had been comfortable with.

Shortly after Marion and I met, which was eight years before she died, she told me that she had had a serious depression and tried to kill herself when she was in graduate school. She left graduate school and lived in Europe for a couple of years and then came back to the States and spent probably eight or ten years under the care of a psychiatrist, with medications and therapy and that kind of thing, through her twenties. She was not finding that her mood was getting any better or that she was feeling any more positive about

Victoria Alexander, *In the Wake of Suicide: Stories of the People Left Behind.* San Francisco, CA: Jossey-Bass, 1991.
Copyright © 1991 by Victoria Alexander. Reproduced by permission of John Wiley & Sons, Inc.

life. So she had shock treatments on an outpatient basis for, I guess, a six-week period. And then after that, she just decided that she had to do something. Her boyfriend was very supportive through this whole thing. They'd been going together for about five years. So she decided that what she needed to do was get married. She got married and had two boys, Andrew and Samuel.

About eight years later, her sister committed suicide. Following her sister's suicide, Marion began addressing the issues in her life in a more direct way. That's when she came out sexually. She left her husband in 1980. It was a very painful and difficult time for her. There was a lot of stress and acclimation. She was always talking about how depressed she was and about not wanting to live anymore. And my response was always, "How could you consider doing something like that to me or to the boys, knowing what it does, having experienced losing your sister?"

ENDURING CHRONIC PAIN

Then she developed fibromyalgia, which is a joint and muscle disorder that is chronic but not debilitating in the same way that arthritis is. She was in constant pain from irritable bowel syndrome, which she had developed shortly after her sister committed suicide. So we were dealing with a woman who had a very restricted diet, was in constant physical pain, and was still struggling with depression. She would have periods of being able to cope and then periods of not being able to cope and function. Six or eight months before she died, we started doing a major renovation on the house. She would periodically say to me, "I can't live anymore. You'd be better off without me." And I would say, "How can you possibly say that?" I tried all the usual reasoning tactics to make her understand and appreciate how much the boys and I cared for her and how much we needed her in our lives.

In the spring, around April or May, I got a phone call from her at work, and she was hysterical. She said, "I'm losing my grip. I can't function." I said, "Well, I'll meet you. Where do you want me to meet you?" I left work and picked up some flowers and met her at a park and basically chased her around the pond while she was just hysterical. She ended up sitting in the middle of the path at the pond, sobbing. I didn't understand what was happening. I had no idea. I was very affectionate and tried to be supportive. We went home and had dinner, and she seemed to feel better.

ATTEMPTS AT THERAPY

We decided that the way we were going to address this was for me to go to therapy with her and give her support. We went in to see her psychiatrist, and that was the first time that I heard that she was clinically diagnosed as having a mood disorder. I'd never been aware of that before. I just thought that this was a cyclical thing, and some times were better than others. I hadn't really understood, and she had never really told me. The doctor was explaining this whole thing to both of us and what the future was going to be like. I'm sitting there saying, "That's fine, that's fine, as long as I can understand it, as long as we can educate ourselves about it and Marion understands that I'm here for her and that, by my coming, we can break the isolation that she feels with the illness." We had also decided that once I became comfortable with understanding and being able to support her, we would include the boys, so that the family could understand, because we were always very affected by the ups and downs.

Before she died, she was missing a lot of work. I would get very impatient—"You have to get up. You have to go. You can't stay here. It's just going to get worse." When we went to see the psychiatrist about it, the last thing she said to Marion as we were walking out the door was, "Do you feel suicidal? Are you okay?" That was a relief to me, because it made me understand that Marion had talked about killing herself in a clinical setting, as well as talking about it at home. It wasn't a secret. And Marion said, "No, I'm fine." When we left, I was feeling very positive, although I was physically exhausted and drained. This was the most difficult period we'd been through. For a month before she died, she was eating baby food. She could not digest food anymore and was losing a tremendous amount of weight and had been missing a lot of work and complaining about pain.

MARION GIVES UP

We went to the movies with Andrew, her older son, that Friday night. Samuel, the younger one, was going on a canoeing trip in Maine and had called us when he arrived there. So everyone was connected. Everyone knew what was happening, where everyone else was.

The next day, Andrew and I were working outdoors. Marion was out doing grocery shopping. I came inside later, and she was sobbing. I said, "What's wrong?" She said she wasn't feeling well and didn't know what to do. I called Andrew in, and both of us were comforting her. Then I left the two of them alone. When he came outdoors, I went back into the house. I said, "I think it's important that Andrew be able to comfort you and be part of your illness and understand it." And I asked her if that was okay. Later, Marion was upstairs, and I had to do some errands. I was walking out the front door, and I said, "I'm going to the store. You going to come down and say good-bye to me?" She came down and gave me a kiss and said, "I love you." And I said, "Just hang in there. We're both tired. We have two weeks off. We'll just relax." I was trying to be very reassuring.

When I came back, there was a note from Andrew saying that she had been in a car accident and the police were looking for her. The police had come and picked him up at the house. The accident had occurred just a quarter of a mile from the house, down at the end of the street, around this back country road. So I got in the car and drove down there. Her car was not there, but the police were. Apparently, she had gone into three trees with the car, was injured, bleeding from her face, and ran from the scene. Someone who had been traveling behind her chased her and said, "Are you okay?" And she said, "I'm fine. I live around the corner. Leave me alone," and ran from him. After I had driven back to the house and the police had driven Andrew back, I said to him, "Andrew, there's something you have to know. Your mother is suicidal. We've got to find her." I got in the car and went screaming into the woods, looking for her. We couldn't find her.

There were search parties out all night long. They kept grilling me: Did she drink? Did she do this? Did she do that? No, no, no, no. Around three or four in the morning, I remembered that when we came back from the movie the night before, she wouldn't come to bed. She was out in the kitchen, working from her briefcase. I remembered her preoccupation with her briefcase. So I went out to the closet in the kitchen and found it. Inside there was a note, a suicide note, addressed to me and written to the boys and myself. And there were manila folders for every aspect of her life—her insurance, her personal effects, bank accounts, everything. I didn't tell the police that I'd found a suicide note.

At dawn, they called in the state police dogs and searched the woods for her. They didn't find anything. Then they called the troops from the air base and sent search parties out. Around ten in the morning, they sent state police helicopters out and were scanning the whole area. And the whole time I had this note. I kept thinking, "If we could just find her, maybe she's unconscious from the injury to the head."

39

FINDING THE BODY AND SAYING GOOD-BYE

Around ten thirty in the morning, the lieutenant came down the street in the patrol car and said, "I think we've found her." So I jumped in the car, and he said, "I think everything's okay." We started heading toward a recreational pond down the street from the house. All of a sudden, he shut the radio off and said, "I don't think it's good news." We arrived at the pond, and they were putting her into a body bag. They'd found her under the float on the far side of the pond. I had been at that pond three or four times, all of us had, during the night. But there's a town side, which is the beach part, and then the other side, where nobody goes. That's where she was. The policeman came back and said to me, "Someone has to identify the body." And I said, "I can't do that." So I described some jewelry I'd given her. And he went back and said, "It's her." Then a female police officer came over, got in the car, and couldn't get it started. She was hysterical. She said, "Are you a family member?" And I said, "Yes." She said, "Well, you're going to find out anyway." I said, "What am I going to find out?" She said, "Her wrists were slashed."

The boys and I made all the arrangements for the memorial service ourselves, as a family, which I think was essential, and we were together through the whole thing. We selected poetry and other readings. Each piece would be identified, and the final words would be, "With the reading of this piece, Catherine says good-bye . . . Andrew says good-bye . . . Samuel says good-bye." And we selected the music that would follow. I'll never understand how the three of us made that happen, how we were ever able to come together and go through that process. I have no idea where the thoughts came from, I have no idea where the music came from, I have no idea where the energy came from.

The day of the service, the three of us went upstairs, and the boys ironed my dress while I showered. We came down the stairs together and went to the service after everyone was already in the church. There was a real feeling of connectedness among the three of us. There were people from all aspects of Marion's life at the service: from her professional life, her personal life, her family life. I don't think people knew all the facets of her, because we all shared so many different connections with her. We really made an effort in the service to take all the fragments and make them whole again and share with people our view of who Marion was. And I know that we were successful in doing that.

People were very vigilant the first week and following that. They were at the house. But it was bizarre. It was as though people couldn't accept the truth, not only the truth about her death and the fact that she had really died but also the truth about how it happened. A few very close friends knew the truth and couldn't accept it. The majority of people did not know—and to this day do not know—what really happened. I know it was very painful for people. Marion's pictures were around the house. But I don't understand why they couldn't cope. Some friends made a real effort to continue to stay connected, and other people ran like hell. They just couldn't connect anymore, didn't know what to say and didn't know what to do.

COPING WITH THE LOSS

I couldn't focus on anything for probably six or eight months. I could listen to music, but I couldn't listen to voices. It was as though there was too much noise in voices, and I'd just block it out. So I'd watch Windham Hill videos. The stereo system had been disconnected because of the construction in the house, and that's the first thing we put together after Marion's death. We played things we thought would be comforting or soothing to listen to.

I went through a period of real trauma thinking that what had happened to Marion was going to happen to me. Fortunately, I was seeing a therapist who was able to say, "Listen, you're thirty-five years old. You have shown no signs of any kind of clinical mental disorder. You're not schizophrenic; you're not depressed. You're situationally depressed because of what's happened, but you've been able to function. I can say with a reasonable amount of certainty that you're probably going to be okay." That was a relief to me. I didn't have to worry that I was somehow going to get to a place where I wouldn't be able to manage my life anymore and that the only alternative I would think I had was to kill myself.

The day after we found Marion, the boys and I were sitting in her psychiatrist's office. We went to see her psychiatrist again the day after the memorial service and then saw a family therapist for the rest of the summer together and basically tried to work through the issues and the realities of what had happened. Her younger son, Samuel, was going off to college as a freshman in September—this was July—so I got him ready and took him to school. He was fine for the first week or two, and then he started to crash. He saw a counselor at school, and that seemed to be better. Probably on a daily basis he was calling me. We were all very needy at that time. Marion's older son, Andrew, tried very hard just to go on. Samuel and I were the basket cases, and Andrew was trying to be strong. He said to us, "I feel as though I said good-bye to Mom the day of the service." I had some real concerns about him, because two summers before that, he had been anorexic and was in therapy for almost a year, working through this eating disorder, which is a form of suicidal behavior. I felt that he was really repressing and didn't quite know what to do. I did what I could. I stayed in constant communication with the kids, let them know that I was there, and made sure that we had time together.

BLOWN AWAY

I was completely blown away and didn't want to live anymore myself and had gotten the message from every clinical person I had spoken to, "You can't kill yourself. That's not an option for you. You've got to stay alive for these kids. They cannot deal with that kind of loss." I'd get angry and say, "Why do I?" And I kept struggling along and verbalizing my frustration with therapists and with the boys and trying to understand why I was left in this situation. I was a coparent, but I wasn't the primary parent.

I tried to talk to the boys' father after Marion died. I said to him, "We have to think about what's important for these boys. It's obvious that we are going to have a relationship, and you and I need to work out the logistics of doing that, because I don't want the boys to feel as if they have to choose. We should be able to coexist." He said, "Those boys are fine. They're strong." He had no idea that his son was anorexic, no idea that his son was seeing a therapist at school. These were all things that Marion and I had assumed responsibility for, and now I'm assuming it, on my own, for the boys. Every time there was a crisis or a decision to be made, Marion and I dealt with it, and I've continued to deal with it since Marion's death.

I joined a suicide survivors' group and met a woman whose husband had killed himself seven years earlier. I found that I had a lot in common with her. She has two children who are the same ages as Samuel and Andrew. We were both struggling with the same issues and having a tremendous amount of difficulty understanding how someone could kill herself or himself. The other people in the group had lost blood relatives—father, brother—and they seemed to have an easier time understanding and expressed some insight into that kind of depression. And Sam and Andrew have said that they can understand a little bit that kind of desperation and depression. That's something that I still go over and over again in my mind: I don't understand it. I can't get around it and accept that it's a possibility.

DECIDING TO LIVE AND GO ON

I remember meeting a man at a restaurant about five or six months after Marion died. We somehow ended up sitting on the same side of the table and started chatting. He asked me what I was doing, and I mentioned having lost Marion. This man had never seen me before. He put his arm around me and said, "I want you to know that it's not your fault." He was a retired college professor and had tried to kill himself a year before that. He said, "You don't understand. Marion didn't even know you existed when she was at that place. She wasn't thinking about you, she wasn't thinking about the children, she wasn't thinking about anything other than escape." He gave me, just in that encounter, something else to try to hold on to, to keep going with.

The five months from Marion's death until Christmas were like a white-knuckle ride of terror, but once we made it through that period, we started somehow to have some faith that we could make it through other things—her birthday, the anniversary of her death, our birthdays.

The boys and I have tried to stay connected with one another—to find a way of letting go and making Marion a part of our lives in a positive way, not in a way that feels like a burden and a shame that will never go away. We're trying very hard to make her death something that we can live with. All three of us—and we've said this to one another—have made the decision to live and go on. It may be shitty at times, but we're going to do it. And I think that's a really important decision to have made, because Marion certainly showed us that there are other alternatives.

Wives of Vietnam Veteran Suicide Victims

by Penny Coleman

Post-traumatic stress disorder (PTSD) is a psychological ailment that often manifests in people who have suffered life-threatening experiences such as military combat, a catastrophic natural disaster, a terrorist attack, a serious accident, or a violent assault. Symptoms of this condition include sleeping difficulties, feelings of detachment or estrangement, and frequent reliving of the experience through flashbacks and nightmares. PTSD often occurs in conjunction with other disorders like depression and drug abuse, and, if the symptoms proceed unchecked, they can degrade a victim's daily life. Frequently, PTSD impairs a person's ability to function properly in a social or familial environment, increasing the degree of detachment and estrangement felt by the sufferer. Suicide is often the tragic result of this inability to reconnect with other individuals.

In the following narrative, Penny Coleman, a photographer and educator, discusses her response to the suicide of her husband, Daniel, in the wake of his bout with PTSD. Central to her story is the issue of assigning blame for her husband's death. Coleman, at the time of her husband's suicide, was unaware of PTSD and its effects on those who suffer from it. She claims that once she learned of this ailment, her grief became manageable and she began to discover an entire community of other women who had lost their husbands to this mental disorder. Since that time, Coleman has been active in organizing the Vietnam War Widows Project, a support group that seeks to educate the public about PTSD and its effects on women who lived in its shadow.

It is only recently that I have begun to think of myself as a Vietnam War widow. In the '70s, when Daniel and I met, we were just two young photographers, trying to make a go of a difficult marriage. Daniel had recently returned from Vietnam. He told funny stories about escapades during R & R [rest and relaxation], but he refused to talk about anything more serious. He slept too much, drank too much, smoked too much marijuana and held me much too close. He was hurt in ways I couldn't fix. When I tried to distance myself, he tried to kill himself. When I found him and called the paramedics, he screamed at me from his hospital bed that he did not consider that act a favor. I left him, headed home to New York and was already married to someone else when his sister called to tell me that he had taken his own life. I have no memory of what I felt. I wasn't surprised. I suppose I was numb. I didn't go to the funeral.

SEARCHING FOR A PLACE TO LAY THE BLAME

It never occurred to me to blame the war for what had happened to us. I tried to blame him but ended up blaming myself. If only I had been kinder, more patient, less self-absorbed, quicker to notice and identify trouble. I can find more compassion for us both from this distance. I now see that he was just a kid who tried to stay alive in a situation that exploded all the rules he had ever lived by, and that he was too sorry and too ashamed to imagine starting over. I know now that I was over my head in a situation I neither understood nor controlled, and that I was sincerely doing the best I could. But at the time I believed his death was my fault.

Denial is often a first response to traumatic events. Numbing is another. I submerged myself in my new life and never spoke about that piece of my past. But the guilt, the shame and the fear that what had happened once might happen again continued insidiously to infect my life and my relationships. It was not until the late '80s, when I encountered the literature on Vietnam and Post-Traumatic Stress Disorder (PTSD), that the absolute shell began to crack. The symptomology had an eerie familiarity—and, in the suggestion that perhaps it had not all been my fault, I found some room to breathe. Finding my way to the surface has been a long and slow process. It would be dishonest to suggest that the process is complete.

In many ways, my life since Daniel died has been the life we planned together. I worked as a photographer for the *New York Times* and other papers. I had two children and began to teach photography at a university. Now I am finally opening a door I myself closed years ago. After twenty-two years, and in light of what I have learned about PTSD, I am beginning to explore, with other women, the parameters of a grief that many of us suffered in silence, shame and isolation.

RELIEF IN THE COMPANY OF FELLOW "WIDOWS"

We all know that there are some 58,000 names on the Vietnam Memorial Wall. Yet by the late 1980s, some media reports estimated that the number of Vietnam veteran suicides had exceeded the number of combat deaths. This number includes those who never left a note, who simply drove the family car into a tree or who died of an overdose, the ones that some families prefer to call "accidents." There was no community available to the women who were left behind. . . . Drawing on my skills as a photographer and oral historian, I have been locating and interviewing other Vietnam War widows whose loved ones' names are not inscribed on the Wall, whose loved ones were those other, more hidden deaths. I am learning to listen well this time, with compassion for all of us, for what we didn't know, for the help we were never offered, for the shattered lives and the heroism of those who managed to go on. I want to hear what they told themselves, what they told their children, where they found comfort, how they survived.

Learning about PTSD and learning to call myself a Vietnam War widow has helped me to understand that my experience is not unique. I have learned, for example, that I was not alone in being excluded from what Daniel was going though. None of the women I have spoken to heard more than fragments of their partners' traumatic war memories. It was not that I didn't try hard enough or listen well enough, but that I was home and sanctuary and the last place it would be safe to risk exposing a shame.

And I have learned, with some probing, that when survivors talk about overcoming guilt, they are not just talking about omissions, what we wish we might have said or done. Sometimes we are talking about commissions, things that we did that were selfish, cruel and disloyal. I behaved badly when Daniel most needed my help. Some of my memories from those days are tawdry. Only now am I learning to forgive the young woman who flailed and raged and came up with solutions that hurt us both.

DISCOVERING THE BENEFITS OF SELF-EXAMINATION

And then there is something I share with those women who chose their partners after they came home from the war: the question, what was it in our histories that drew us to such wounded souls? Even if the damage was unavailable and unacknowledged, it was

46

surely there below the surface, festering. Could we not feel it, intuit it? That is a question for each of us. For myself, I know that I married what I most feared and least understood: a mirror image of my own despair and the comfort I found in the possibility of suicide. It was always my escape of last resort, the reason I felt free to choose another day, the tactic I used to avoid feeling trapped in my life. My fascination with suicide and with Daniel's frailty had a distinctly morbid quality. I mirrored and shared Daniel's suicidal tendencies, picked at them, on some subconscious level, to see what would happen. I tested and teased at his hold on life the way a miner brings a canary into a mine.

And then there was the hubris that claimed responsibility. If I could control people and events, if I had the power to make things happen, then the world was not such a terrifying place. Believing that I could have prevented Daniel's death was less frightening than knowing I could not. If it was my fault then, then perhaps I could make myself adequate to future challenges, be good enough, wise enough, healthy enough. It was magic thinking—and megalomania— to believe that, if I could just be a better person, the world would right itself.

Even now, knowing what I do, it is a struggle to put aside that sense that I am responsible for Daniel's death. It has taken me twenty-odd years, two beloved children and a lot of therapy to decide to claim my life, to love it, to embrace the richness of its joy and its pain. When my children were born, I wanted to love them fiercely and well. They made me want to live, to really live, to risk. I am still afraid my fears are contagious. I am occasionally afraid that I am contagious. But the ways I wish it had been otherwise, that I had been otherwise, are just that: only wishes. Forgiveness has been largely about healing myself and, through that process, finding a way to grieve.

Coping with a Father's Suicide

by Tammi Landry

In the narrative that follows, Tammi Landry explains the unexpected twist her life took upon learning the news of her father's suicide. Her father served as an Indiana State Police detective for nearly thirty years. As Landry says, he was the type of person who enjoyed protecting others and making the world a better place. Therefore, when she learned that he had taken his own life, the news came as a great shock. Landry knew her father to be a strong and hardworking man; she did not believe he was capable of such an act.

While Landry says that she does not know the exact reason why her father committed suicide, she explains that he may have been involved in illegal activities centered around an auto dealership of which he was part owner. Landry believes that her father was not a criminal, but that the misfortune of being connected to criminal activity may have shamed him enough to take his life.

Tammi Landry has since become a founder and executive director of a chapter of the American Federation for Suicide Prevention in Ann Arbor, Michigan. Her work helps further the healing of those who have been afflicted with the grief of losing a loved one to suicide.

When I was in my late 20s and dreading heading into my early 30s, all of my thirty-something friends would tell me how much more they preferred being in their 30s. Something about being 30 made them feel really "grown up," like they had finally arrived at adulthood. Somehow, turning 30 was like a light coming into their lives, helping to guide them towards better decision-making and a more realistic approach to real life.

Less than one month before I turned 31, my father shot himself

Tammi Landry, "My Father's Suicide," www.afsp.org. Reproduced by permission of the author.

in the head with a .45 caliber Beretta handgun. My friends were certainly right about one thing: heading into my 30s definitely propelled me straight into adulthood. And it made me much more aware of a need to grow up and start acting more mature, even if his death made me feel just like a little girl again.

THE WORST PHONE CALL OF MY LIFE

I remembered that gun from my childhood. He kept it under his side of the bed, just in case he would ever need it in the middle of the night to protect our family. That gun was in our lives every day and every night, and I never even gave it a second thought. My dad was an Indiana State Police detective for almost 27 years. I can remember always being proud of him for the work he had done to make the world a better place to live. He wasn't a huge man, maybe six feet tall on a good day, but had a large chest and muscular arms, and he always seemed like a giant to me. There wasn't a day in my life that I didn't know he was always out there somewhere protecting me. All of that changed the day I got the worst phone call of my life.

My mother, Janis, and sister, Jan, had come to Michigan to visit for a weekend, where I lived with my husband, Mike. We had planned to be together for Jan's 26th birthday. Around 9:00 A.M. the phone rang. The man on the other end of the line told me his name and that he was from the Indiana State Police. The man asked for my mother after I confirmed that I was the daughter of Sgt. Rick Irvin. I immediately went downstairs and gave the phone to my mother. I remember feeling confused as to why he would call my house to ask for my mom. I thought, "*Why not tell me what is happening?*" I'm 30 years old. I'm all grown up now.

My mom took the phone into another room and Mike went with her. I was in the living room with Jan, who had already begun moaning in a way that I had never heard before. I kept repeating, "I think he's just hurt or sick or something. We'll just need to go visit him. Don't cry. He's just hurt or sick. We'll just go visit him." Jan wouldn't stop moaning. She was on the floor rocking back and forth. I wanted her to stop acting as if he was dead. My big, strong, indestructible dad was not going to be dead.

My mom came into the living room and asked us to sit down. Jan was completely hysterical at this point, but I sat down, still acting as if I knew I'd be seeing my dad in a hospital bed in just a few hours. I calmly asked my mom to tell us what was going on. She said the words I will never forget as long as I live, "Your father died this morning." Jan began screaming and rocking back and forth on the floor once again. I don't remember feeling anything at all except confused. Jan was screaming, "What happened, mom?! What happened?!" My mom, with anger in her eyes, stated, "He shot himself."

My mind stopped for a moment, and my whole body went numb. I remember my eyes blinking almost uncontrollably, and I became more confused and felt as if something wasn't right, like my mom had to be mistaken. Police officers don't kill themselves. What was I going to do now? So much for entering into my 30s and feeling "all grown up." At that moment, I felt more like a little girl than ever.

A LITTLE HISTORY

My parents divorced after 23 years of marriage. I never remember their marriage being a happy one, and I remember my dad sitting down a few different times with Jan and me when we were very small and telling us that he was going away for a little while because "he and mommy were not getting along very well." My dad was normally either incredibly happy or devastatingly sad most of his life: there were very few in-betweens. When my parents separated for the first time, I think I was about 11 years old. I remembered my dad being very depressed and hearing my parents talk about it late one night. I thought that I remembered him saying that he wanted to kill himself. I have always known that was the reason my mother decided to take him back. She feared that he would end his life if she left him. When he moved back in with us, it really didn't get any better. Eventually, they divorced.

A couple of years prior to his death, he had moved to southern Indiana and bought a beautiful piece of land with a little house on it to live. He had a fairly large pond in his backyard, and he lived with his favorite companion, Shadow, a black labrador retriever Jan and I had bought for him for one of his birthdays. I really thought he was finally happy. Little did I know that he was involved in a lot more than I ever knew, and that his life was far from happy.

UNDER THE MICROSCOPE

After hearing the news about my father's death, my mom, my sister and my husband and I did not know what to do. Did we need to start calling people? I was unable to pick up the telephone and speak with anyone right away. My mom called my dad's best friend, who was also a police officer. He informed us that there was something else going on that we should know. My father had invested some money in a small car dealership, along with a friend of his, a retired police officer from southern Indiana. The day before my father shot himself, the Bureau of Alcohol, Tobacco and Firearms (ATF) and the Indiana State Police raided the auto dealership. There were stolen guns and drugs found there. My dad's best friend wanted us to know that this would be in the Indiana newspapers and on the television news. He made it perfectly clear how well he knew our father and that my father would never have known of illegal activities taking place at the dealership. He wasn't sure, but he thought that dad was a part owner of this business.

I remember thinking that this kind of thing doesn't happen to regular people. Nobody has a father who invests money in some stupid car dealership, finds out the manager was dealing drugs, and then kills himself! I was sick at the thought that people would think of my dad as a criminal. He had dedicated his life to arresting people who dealt drugs, and now he was going to be associated with those same kinds of people. I began thinking that he must have been so devastated by the fact that he would have been linked to something like this, that that was the reason he decided to take his life.

Jan and my mother arrived home in Indiana later that afternoon. Sure enough, the top story on the Indianapolis news was the raid at the dealership and the suicide of the part owner, a 26-year veteran of the Indiana State Police. They flashed a huge picture on the television of my dad that filled the entire screen. Although the news media didn't actually come out and say my father was a criminal, they made it seem as if he shot himself because he must have been dealing drugs and buying and selling stolen guns and cars behind the scenes at this auto dealership. I was heartbroken to think that this would be the ending to my father's impeccable career as a proud and brilliant detective.

SAYING GOODBYE

I hated the thought of having to greet people at the visitation. I was consumed, almost obsessed, with the thought of having people looking at me and feeling sorry, but at the same time thinking, *"What a nutcase he must have been to do this,"* not to mention the fact that the majority of the people coming to offer their condolences to my family and I were also thinking that my dad was guilty of drug dealing, gun smuggling and auto theft.

Since my dad shot himself just above the temple on the right side of the head, we were able to have an open casket. I was mortified at the thought of seeing my father's dead body in a coffin, but believed that it probably would help the "healing process" if I did see him. I didn't think the body lying in the casket looked at all like my dad. His body was bloated and his face was huge. His eyes and mouth were closed and he didn't look peaceful or angry or sad. He looked totally fake, like an imposter.

We had a couple of pictures of my dad there, so when I wanted to look at my dad, instead of looking in the coffin, I looked at the pictures. To this day, I still do not remember many of the people who came; it was almost as if I was in a cloud or a dream, like it really never happened. The funeral the next day was much more difficult, and seemed a bit more real.

I dreaded the beginning of the ceremony because I knew that this would be the last time I would be able to tell my father goodbye. I really didn't think I could let him go. When they took the coffin out of the sanctuary, my heart felt as if it was being ripped apart. I knew this was the end. I tried to tell him goodbye, but the words wouldn't come out of my mouth. Jan was thinking the same thing because she looked at me with the most saddened pair of eyes and said, "I'm not ready to let him go."

As we followed the coffin outside, I saw the most impressive scene: 40 or 50 policemen dressed in their formal uniforms saluting my father's coffin as it was being put into the hearse. Words could not describe how I felt at that moment. The despair and grief were accompanied by an overwhelming feeling of respect for my father and his profession, as well as for every single officer there who honored him by saluting his casket. In the distance, the television reporters and their cameras zoomed in on the sad faces of my family and I. That night, we were once again one of their top stories.

BACK TO NORMAL?

I think the strangest thing about all of this is that people seem to expect you to just bounce back to normal after something like this happens. My first week back to work was overwhelming. I had no idea how to begin doing my job; I felt I'd been away so long. My life had changed in a matter of moments, and now I was supposed to jump right back into my "normal" life and carry on, which just seemed completely bizarre.

Every day I tried my best to go to work and concentrate on my job. I always really liked what I did. I got to plan events and work as a marketing manager for a small company, which was really a lot of fun, most of the time. However, after my father died, my heart just wasn't in it the way it was before. I realized that my priorities had changed and that the little things that used to bother me no longer did.

Suicide never leaves you. It follows you from friend to friend, from job to job, from house to house. There's always a constant reminder in the back of your head that you're just so much different than most everyone else around you.

HEALING BEGINS

A couple of months after dad died, Mike and I took a trip to California. We stayed in a beautiful place, near the beach, with a health club and shopping nearby. I remember taking a walk just a couple of hours after I had gotten out of bed and worked out at the health club. I was enjoying the citrus and floral smell of California and the feeling of the warm sun on my face when I realized that for two hours that day, I hadn't yet thought about my dad or the way he died. I was relieved for a few seconds, but then quickly became overcome with guilt. I suppose I felt guilty for enjoying myself too much when I thought I should have been thinking about my father, his life and his death. I thought to myself, *"When am I ever going to be able to have fun again without feeling this way?"* I never thought it could be possible.

Understanding That Suicidal Depression Is Hereditary

by Treva Gordon

Surviving the suicide of a parent is a difficult challenge. In the following narrative, Treva Gordon relates her story of coping with the suicide of her mother, Joy. Gordon portrays her mother as a vibrant and robust woman who suffered many hardships throughout her life, including the suicide of her own father. While Gordon was aware that her mother suffered from depression at times, she claims that she never thought her mother would be capable of taking her own life because she seemed so strong and unshakeable.

In dealing with her grief, Gordon explains that her own life fell apart, causing her to reach a point where suicide appeared to be a way out of her depression. Through therapy, however, Gordon learned that some medical experts link suicidal depression to hereditary factors. That knowledge steeled Gordon's determination not to let depression rob her of her own life, and she was thereafter able to put her life back together.

Her name was Joy and that's what she was. Once she stepped into your life you never forgot her. She was respected and loved by everyone who met her. Throughout her life she had endured heartache and tragedy. She lost her father, sister, and two brothers in the prime of their lives. Her nineteen-year marriage ended in divorce. She suffered periodically from depression. Through all her hardship and struggles, she pulled herself up. Her determination to survive was tremendous, her spirit so strong. She was only fifty-seven when she died.

She raised five daughters. She was my light when I needed direction, my rock. I married young and found myself struggling to keep the marriage together while working and raising a family. Mom supported me—emotionally and in many practical ways. I named my first daughter after my mother, as I wanted a part of her grandma to be with her always. My mother was always a proud and active grandma. Thus, Mom's reaction when I had my third child was particularly strange. She didn't get a present for the new baby, she didn't call as often, she seemed preoccupied by trivial things. I was so wrapped up in the new baby that I didn't read much into these changes.

IN THE WAKE OF AN UNEXPECTED SUICIDE

Then five weeks after the baby was born, Mom killed herself. At first, I was filled with anger. How could she have truly loved us? How could she leave her own grandchildren? Why couldn't she make it one more day? Wasn't our love enough to make her stay alive?

My three children (ages fourteen, six, and five weeks) kept me from falling apart. I had to be strong for them. They had depended on their grandma as much as I had. I never hid the truth from them. I never gave them the horrible details—but I never lied. Any questions that they had deserved an honest answer. Always, the hardest question to face was "Why, Mommy?" How could I respond when I too searched so hard for the answer? I told them that she was sad, so sad that the pain she felt was unbearable. My answer haunted me later, sometimes even today. If I was having an extremely hard day, my precious children would sometimes ask, "Mommy, are you sad? Are you sad like Grandma was?" I could see the fear in their eyes. I could only reassure them time and time again that I was okay, that sometimes people do feel sad but they are all right. Other times my children were so angry they would scream out at their grandma. Punches thrown at doors and walls would express the depth of the anger. One child had been particularly close to my mother. She was the buddy, the soul mate. Now she was gone. No one could fill her shoes. Shortly after her death, this child was so upset at Grandma's betrayal that the words, "I'm going to kill myself. Grandma did, so can I," came out. I was devastated. A caring counselor came to our rescue and helped the children sort out their complex emotional reactions.

Somehow we made it through the firsts: Christmas, birthdays, all those holidays that Mom made more special. I sheltered myself in my home. As long as my kids were around me and my sisters nearby, I felt safe. Nothing could happen to them if they were close by. In the beginning, it seemed I drowned in tears. But slowly, very slowly, the pain in my heart began to lessen. The baby brought joy to us all. She reaffirmed life. She was a new beginning. Going through the everyday routine of life became less of a struggle. Laughter became real again.

But while I fought to keep my children and myself going, my marriage fell apart. Our marriage was fragile before my mom's death. It was not strong enough to survive the demands of grieving. Within two years, I had lost my mom and my marriage. It wasn't long after that that I almost lost myself.

STARTING OVER AND BREAKING DOWN

After the divorce, I decided to go back to school. I had to earn a decent living. I had to start all over with my life. The anxiety of leaving the safety of my home and family overwhelmed me. After pulling myself up day after day, I just could not pull anymore. I was physically and emotionally exhausted. I would try to sleep, but I would wake up every hour, my heart racing madly. I tried to eat, but the food choked me. For the first time in my life, I had lost my will, my spirit. I wanted to crawl in a dark corner and be left alone. I started crying on a Thursday. The next day, I was still crying. My sister took me to a mental health clinic. I hadn't stopped crying. The nurse was wonderful. She knew I was having a breakdown severe enough to require hospitalization. I had no insurance, no money. She found a hospital that had a community bed for people in situations like mine. It allowed me to get the help I needed at no cost.

The doctor who was assigned to me came in that night. He pronounced me suicidal. He said I needed to face the fact that I was like my mother. I argued with him. I got mad at him. I was not like her. I WANTED TO LIVE. But slowly I realized that what he was trying to say to me had some truth to it. A propensity to depression is hereditary. My mother's father had taken his life. My mother fought all her life with depression. It finally won. But I was determined to break the cycle. I reached out for help. Mental illness is not a shameful thing. What's shameful is not getting help. I can now say I have a small idea of the hell your mind can put you through. I lived through a relatively short episode of what my mother experienced. But I reached out for help and found hope.

THE LONG JOURNEY BACK

It's been a long journey back—but a worthwhile one that has enabled me to live my life to the fullest. After my recovery, I enrolled in a vocational-technical school and received a certificate in building maintenance. I was the first female to graduate with this degree. I now have a dream job with the National Park Service. I am learning to love again. I have met a wonderful man who holds me when the tears fall. He knows my grief and understands my life. My children are surviving right beside me. They lost their grandma, their dad, and their way of life. To say it has been easy would be a lie. To say we don't struggle at times with Mom's death, even today, would be an even greater lie. But now when we talk about Grandma, it is with fondness and smiles more than anger and tears.

I am in control of my life now. My children have seen and know the determination it takes to keep going. I hope I have given them the strength to persevere when all seems lost. Through all our struggles we have survived together. My spirit has survived along with me, and I see that spirit in my children. I believe this spirit belongs to my mother. It's the part of her that has been with us all along.

Learning the Lessons of My Father's Suicide

by James A. Gessner

In the narrative that follows, James A. Gessner provides an account of his reaction to his father's suicide. Gessner describes how he followed in his father's footsteps in many aspects of his own life—becoming an airline pilot and suffering from both depression and serious alcoholism. However, Gessner explains that the emotional instability that finally debilitated his father and led to his unfortunate demise did not have the same effect on Gessner himself.

Gessner claims that he learned many life lessons from his father and that he used this knowledge to help him overcome the turmoil that characterized his own life. He desires to remember his father in a positive light, to teach his children the lessons he learned in childhood, and to remain open to the ongoing healing process that he undertook to deal with his grief.

M y father was an airline pilot and I was proud of him for doing what he loved. His parents had not wanted him to pursue aviation, but he persevered. His lesson taught me a lot about life: Do what you love. I remember my father having lots of energy and really enjoying himself when I was young. He sang and whistled. He had a happy marriage and two loving children. But my father drank too much even then.

LIVING WITH ALCOHOLISM

He wasn't abusive when he drank. Somehow, this made it easier to ignore. My mom was concerned, but not overly so. At some point in his life his problems began to overcome him. He began to drink more. In time, his stress levels became so high that he had to stop flying. In 1974 he took a disability retirement from his airline. He was told to seek psychiatric help, but he refused. Several years later he said that the prospect of dying was less frightening to him than feeling the emotions he was numbing. He became suicidal. Once he said, "If it wasn't for my wife and children I would kill myself." The statement indicates his love for us, but it also pisses me off. It places a huge burden on the family—be there or Dad will shoot himself. One time when I was arguing with Dad he blurted out, "What do you want me to do . . . kill myself?" Then he walked outside, got in his car, and drove away. He came back that time. But there is still a part of my brain that believes that my strong emotions will cause someone to die. I struggle not to pass this distorted thinking on to my children.

During my teenage years, Dad seldom sang or whistled. He spent a great deal of time sitting in the kitchen and staring out the back window. He drank tea during the day. At night he drank beer or wine and watched TV until very late. I felt neglected and lonely. Since nobody told me what was going on, I thought I was the problem, and I became depressed. Each of us began to exist in our own little worlds. I alternated between denial and contemplating my own suicide. I lived with the fear that Dad would kill himself. Intuitively I knew I had to get out of there.

I first learned about the disease of alcoholism when I was at college. One day a pilot for a major airline came to our school (it was an aviation school) and spoke about his battle with alcoholism and his road to sobriety. Somehow his story penetrated my denial. I didn't seek help for myself right away, but I couldn't shake what that man told me. I finally began my own road to healing at the age of twenty-one . . . twelve years before Dad killed himself.

I often wonder why some people get help and begin living more vibrant lives while others just fade away. Over the last ten years, I was able to talk openly about the pain that I felt with my father and mother. It wasn't easy—skydiving for the first time was less intense. I told my father how hurt I would feel if he killed himself. For the first time in my life, I told him that I loved him. I tried many times to convince him to get help, but he never did.

FINDING SUPPORT

I found out about my dad's death after I stepped off a plane I had copiloted from Detroit to St. Louis. The woman at the crew desk already knew and had set up my trip home. She looked at me with compassion and said, "I'm so sorry." She invited me behind the counter to avail myself of what little privacy there was. A fellow pilot responded with similar sensitivity. These people helped me because they had the strength to face death and were not put off by my intense feelings. They provided compassion, not problem solving; I needed to feel my feelings first and analyze them later. Many people were and are afraid to say anything about my father to me. Saddest of all, my father's family rarely mentions him. I try to speak about my dad first to let them know I am comfortable talking about him, but it doesn't advance the conversation.

One forum in which I can speak openly about my father and my feelings about his death are Survivors of Suicide groups. Hearing the stories of others diminishes my sense of loneliness. I have found that if I miss a meeting or I haven't been able to talk about the suicide for a while I become irritable and tense. It would have been too burdensome to make my wife my entire support system. It was very hard for her to go through this loss with me. Some days, especially when she was sad about her own father who suffers from Alzheimer's disease, she just wasn't able to listen to my pain and sadness. In fairness to her and to us, I have made sure I ask others to listen to me too.

WHAT IT MEANS TO BE A MAN

Part of what I've had to work out during the time since my dad's retirement and eventual suicide is what it means to be a man. In particular, I've needed to learn how to accept my feelings and to allow myself to cry. I feared that if I began to cry I wouldn't be able to stop. To my surprise, my tears have been the pathway to my healing. It has become very important to share my emotions with those who can handle them. When I am able, I let my wife hold me when I cry. Although I first had to overcome anxiety about the response of other men to my tears (I thought I would be perceived as a weak man), I have found letting them see my emotions to be very healing. I've realized that it takes strong men to buck societal norms and do whatever it takes to heal. Part of my motivation to develop healthier coping skills than my father had is my desire not to pass on destructive patterns to a new generation. But, despite all my growth, I am scared that when I become my father's age I will see and feel the type of pain that incapacitated him.

For some time, the most vivid image I had of my father was his exit from this world—an exit terrible in its specifics and its outcome. The pain this image evokes is beyond my capacity to describe. The pain of him dying alone. The pain of him not wanting to be a bother to anyone and his refusal to let people help him. The pain of him not realizing how important his life was. I weep for his inability to know his connection to all people and all things. To help counter this traumatic image, I've concentrated on a memory I have of him from childhood. I was sitting next to him while he was working on a crossword puzzle. He had on a blue corduroy shirt. He smelled of pipe tobacco. Most clearly I remember his breathing. When I remember his breathing a sort of peace comes over me like it did when I was a child. I felt cared for, I felt safe. It is important for me to remember my father by how he lived his life, not by how he left it.

LEARNING LESSONS AND PASSING THEM ON

I often wonder what I can teach my children about the lessons of my childhood and the kind of man my father was. The most important thing I want my new daughter to know is that I love her and care about her. I also want her to know that when parents are sick, it is not her fault. I want to make it clear that she is free to share her feelings with me, even if that feeling is anger with me. As for how and when I will tell her about my father's death, I plan on telling her as soon as she asks or is curious about why she can't see him. We will tell her my dad had a disease that affected how he thought. His disease prevented him from realizing how important he really was to himself, to God, and to us. I will also tell her that he killed himself. Children are more capable of handling the truth than many people give them credit for. (It's the adults I worry about.) I will also share with her the wonderful things my father taught me and how much he loved little children.

I miss my father. Of all my current feelings, missing my father is the strongest. My father will never see any of his grandchildren. I will never be able to see him hold our newborn daughter. I can't hug him. I can't tell him I love him. I miss his laughter. I miss his flying stories. I often wonder why I chose to fly airplanes for a living. I didn't want to follow in my father's footsteps. At least not the depressed father I knew from my teenage years. But, I wonder if I did subconsciously choose it to find out why it once gave my father such joy. When I look with a sense of awe at a beautiful sunset from an airplane, I wonder if my dad can see it with me.

CHAPTER 3

Therapists' Perspectives
on Suicide

A Nurse Counsels a Suicidal Patient

by Jane Bates

In the following article, nurse Jane Bates recalls her experience
with an anonymous suicide attempter while working in the
emergency department of a London Hospital in the 1970s. She
explains that she felt obligated to sit and talk with the young
man after he was put under her care—an act that, as Bates pro-
fesses, was outside of her normal duties as a nurse. Bates states
that she and the other nurses in her department commonly dealt
with attempted suicides, but interaction with the patients was
normally restricted to urgent medical care. Bates, however, tells
how she took a moment to transcend normal procedure and in-
teract with her charge on a more human level. Bates now works
in outpatient care in Hampshire, England.

Over recent years the Thames [River] has been cleansed and re-
vitalized. Now otters gambol on its banks, and fish swim lazily
in its shallows. Before these halcyon days, the river was a foul mid-
den, a stew of spilt fuel, dead dogs and all kinds of noxious effluent.

So the young man I was talking with one rainy evening did not
smell his best, having attempted suicide by leaping in. Fortunately,
he [was] fished out and dumped in our casualty department before
he could drown.

We must have made an odd couple. He, dried out and wrapped
in a blanket but reeking of *eau de* Thames, miserable with regret
and embarrassment—and me in my starched uniform, wearing a hat
resembling a bleached parrot.

It was one of those wet weekday evenings when nothing much
happens in an inner-city A&E [accident and emergency] department. Neither of us was going anywhere for several hours, so we
just sat and talked. Physically he was fine, but emotionally he was
anything but.

"What are you doing?" the senior house officer asked me wearily,

Jane Bates, "All Wrung Out," *Nursing Standard*, vol. 18, August 25, 2004. Copyright © 2004 by *Nursing Standard*.
Reproduced by permission.

meaning to be kind. "There is nothing you can do for people like him. Come and have a cup of tea with the rest of us instead."

I knew what would happen to this patient next. There would be the perfunctory consultation with a psychiatrist in the morning, and then he would disappear into the ether and no one would ever know why, at the tender age of 20—the same age as I was—he had decided to throw himself off Westminster Bridge. They came back time after time, these attempted suicides, and it is no wonder that the A&E old-stagers became cynical. All the while that we were pumping out stomachs or treating the effects of temporary immersion in river water, we were deflected from attending to the accidents and acute illnesses that are the meat and drink of your average casualty department.

CHOOSING TEA OR SYMPATHY

"Surely," I argued timidly, "if someone tries to take their own life they must have psychiatric problems or devastating emotional distress? Should they not be as important as any other patient?" But no one seemed interested. They patted me on the head as though I was their pet idealist and that was that.

So we sat and talked. He had come down to the Big Smoke [London] from Glasgow [Scotland] with his girlfriend who had, after a few months, got bored and left him. He was suddenly all alone in this huge, faceless city. I guessed he could not go home for one reason or another. So, in one terrible moment of despair, he had tried to finish himself off.

I do not know what I expected to achieve by my amateurish attempts at counseling. But one thing I did realize was that the uniform, which I often despised as a barrier between ourselves and our patients, was a verification of my role. It prevented me from getting in too deep.

We must have chatted for several hours, and I never knew what happened to him after that. I just hope he managed to find some reason to keep going, a spark of hope, and somehow I think he did. Whenever I remember that night I ask myself how I would react now, 30 years on and with a zeal that probably flagged its last a long time ago. Would I still be at the young man's side, I wonder? Or in the tearoom with the others who have seen it all before?

A Therapist Loses a Patient to Suicide

by Ellen

In the following article, a social worker named Ellen recounts learning that a patient she had been counseling committed suicide. The patient, a college graduate referred to as Joe in the piece, attempted but failed to take his life once before trying again and succeeding. Ellen's story reveals the strong attachment therapists and patients sometimes create during counseling sessions. Although Ellen did not know Joe well, she admits that she felt guilty for his death and ultimately questioned her own abilities to help those in trouble.

I did the intake evaluation on Joe when he first called to make an appointment at the mental health clinic where I've been working as a social work intern. He was twenty-four and had graduated from college the previous summer. At that point, he was speaking about suicide. I didn't ask all the right questions. It was probably the first intake that I had done in which somebody had expressed any thoughts about suicide. I got off the phone and thought, "I should have asked other questions," and I really wasn't clear what. And then somebody said, "Well, did you give him the hot line number to [the psychiatric hospital]?" And I said, "Oh, no!" It was scary for me. I found out all this information that I should tell him and maybe some more questions that I should ask. I called him back, but there was no answer. This was a Friday afternoon, so there was no way for me to get in contact with him until Monday. It was just scary for me to think that maybe I should have told him more. I looked through the obituary page on Saturday and Sunday, praying that this guy would know what to do if he felt that desperate.

I ended up having Joe assigned to me for therapy. He was a very intense, dependent person. He felt that he wanted to see me more than once a week. He said twice a week. And my inclination was to say okay. As a result, even though it was a short period of time that I met him, it was very intense.

Sometimes you meet people and there's just a connection of some sort. I really can't put it in words. There was just, on my part and it seemed on his part, some kind of nice connection that occurred between the two of us. There was something really likable about this guy. He was very engaging, very articulate. The way he would articulate his thoughts and his feelings had this poetic fashion to it. He had a sense of humor. He was very bright. There were certain issues that I could even identify with, not to the same degree perhaps that he was experiencing them, but some of his issues were issues and feelings that many people who are right out of college would experience.

He would talk a little about suicide, and we contracted, in the sense that he said he would be able to call me or the hospital if need be, if he felt that he would act on his impulses. When I asked him if he knew anybody who had ever attempted or committed suicide, he said no. And then I asked him if anyone in his family ever had, and he said, "Oh, yeah, my brother, ten years ago, attempted suicide." It's interesting how people sometimes make a division between everyone else and their family members.

I was planning to take a week off during Christmas, and Joe was going to visit his family out of state. Even when we were parting, I just never knew what he was going to do or if he would return. I thought he might leave and not come back. It's kind of an odd feeling to say good-bye to somebody and not know if you're ever going to see him again, even though you make an appointment and even though you feel that you're building some type of relationship. There are some people you know are not going to return. But Joe would not return only if he was not going to come back to this state. He was very unhappy living here, and he had a girlfriend out of state. There was no reason to stay. He wasn't here through choice. He was here almost through lack of choice, lack of any other place to be. It's hard to work with somebody when you don't know if he's going to split town the next day.

THE FIRST ATTEMPT

He called during his vacation. I wasn't there, and he talked to my supervisor. He talked about whether he should hospitalize himself. He was talking about feeling depressed. That was a major issue: feeling depressed, feeling loss. There were real identity issues, as far as

"Who am I?" He had great difficulty making choices, taking responsibility. But he didn't hospitalize himself, and he did come back. I contracted with him again, but I was never sure. Of all my clients, he was one I just didn't know. It got to the point where I didn't know what he was going to do when he walked out of the office. It never felt clear. I never felt comfortable. He just wasn't always there. He would go on and on and on with thoughts, but I never felt secure that *he* was secure in what he could do and not do. I talked about him to a variety of people, really looking for somebody else to meet with him. I was an intern. I just wasn't sure, and I was grappling. I was constantly grappling with decisions. It was too big a responsibility. I shared it all with both my supervisors, but no clear decision was ever made. So I just kept moving along and seeing where it went.

[Then one day Joe attempted suicide but survived.] I had seen him earlier that day, and there was no hint. I [found out] about it the next morning. I was devastated. I went over my notes. I looked, looked. What did I miss? I know I had asked if he was okay. I don't really remember that much more of the conversation. I didn't want to go to work. I didn't want to see anybody. I remember speaking to one of my supervisors. What could he say? I was just so distraught. I felt a sense of responsibility. Intellectually, yes, I could say I couldn't have done anything and it wasn't my fault. But I had this pain in my stomach. I felt that I had missed something or I should have done something or I should have gone by my gut a couple of weeks earlier and made sure somebody else saw him. I don't know, I should have done *something*. I remember that day at work, because I had another client come in. All of a sudden, she started talking about feeling depressed and how she'd thought about suicide. I didn't show it to her, but my antennae went up, of course, and a part of me said, "I don't want to hear this. Don't tell me; tell somebody else. Maybe I don't belong in this field." It was so hard to sit with a client and be focused on her issues, because I was having trouble just keeping myself above water.

I talked to people all day. I called my other supervisor. And people said, "You can't do anything about it. You can't change it. It's not your fault. People make these decisions independently of you, and we can't always stop people." But it was really hard to integrate that into my pit, my stomach.

I remember the first phone conversation I had with Joe after his attempt. I told him that the most important thing was that he was alive. He sent out double messages, which included, "I hope you don't get in trouble for what I did." And I responded, "Well, that's nothing for you to worry about. The most important thing is that you're okay." And I used to think, "What the hell was he trying to say to me? What were these double messages? Was he really angry at me and felt I should have done something and wanted me to get into trouble?" I don't know.

He was seeing a psychiatrist [at the hospital] at that point. There was a decision that he was going to continue seeing the psychiatrist after he was discharged, so it seemed like a good idea that we terminate therapy. We probably met three more times. We talked about his suicide attempt. Part of the problem, he said, was that he could contract with people, but he didn't know at that moment that he would be planning on committing suicide or attempting it two hours later. So he could say something at that moment, but his feelings or thoughts could change drastically. I found out later, through his father, that he had bought the hose that he used to try to kill himself before he saw me, on the day he attempted suicide, so he wasn't sharing that piece with me.

He was having a hard time saying good-bye. He said that there were only a few people out there who really knew him and that I was one of them, so that losing me was really tough. He was crying. There was a lot of emotion in that room—ending, saying good-bye, and hoping that he would be able to follow through with the psychiatrist and stick with it and come to peace with some of the issues that were bothering him. Again, there was always this feeling that I didn't know how much truth he was sharing with me at the time. What was just the outer façade? What was he just saying for effect? What was he really feeling? I remember at the end of our last meeting, I asked how much of him he felt was really genuine that day. He said, "A little piece."

WHAT A WASTE

Sometime later, I called the social worker at the hospital about something totally irrelevant to Joe. She was sitting in the office with the psychiatrist, and they had just heard that he had committed suicide. I was silent on the phone. I didn't know what to say. The only words that came out of my mouth were, "He's such an asshole!" What a waste! Why did he do that? There was so much inside him.

He hung himself on the bathroom pipes. And he had seen the psychiatrist the same day or the day before. She also didn't know.

Every time he left the office, she didn't know. Would he be okay? You just never knew with Joe.

I was a wreck. I couldn't believe it. I really didn't believe it in some ways. I didn't want to believe that he had done it. I used to fantasize that I'd see him on the street or he'd call up or come into the office. It just didn't seem possible that he could end his life at age twenty-four and that there was so much promise and so much creativity and so much talent. Through my eyes, he had so much to offer people, and he just couldn't see it. He couldn't see the light at the end of the tunnel. He couldn't see that maybe in two or three years he would feel better. My gut feeling was "Asshole," but I just felt so much sadness for him. And that pain in the gut returned. People used to ask me, "Aren't you angry?" and I'd say, "No." To me it was just such a waste. I felt so sorry for him, that he couldn't see what I saw and what other people saw in him, that he had so much to offer, that he was really special.

I learned that his father had found a suicide note addressed to me. I thought, "I don't really want this." Part of me was afraid that he was blaming me and that he was angry at me, and I just didn't want him to be angry at me. Although the note wasn't dated, they thought that it was probably from the first suicide attempt. He had never made any mention of it. Every day I'd look in my mailbox, waiting for this letter to be sent by Joe's father. That's all I would go to work for, to look in my mailbox and see if the note was there. Finally, it came. I dreaded opening it, but I opened it. It was addressed to me, and it just talked about how much despair he felt and that he was finally making a choice.

TALKING ABOUT IT

I've never been able to cry about it, which seems out of character for me, and I never understood why I wasn't able to express my sadness that way. I just had this pain in my stomach. And I'd get all shaky and upset when I would share it with other people and just be at a loss for words.

I remember after his first attempt I spent the whole next day making all these long-distance phone calls. It was my way of reaching out to people, to talk to people about it. I was just so upset. I talked to a woman who's a social worker and has been somewhat of a mentor. She's one of my mother's friends, and I'm really fond of her. She told me, "Nobody's omnipotent. You have these messianic ideals. We can help people, but sometimes we just can't stop people who really want to go through with it." That was helpful.

About a month after Joe's suicide, or over a month, I presented his case to a group of interns at the clinic. I thought I would be able to do it and that I would be okay about it. What a mistake. I was shaking. I was *so* overwhelmed—such intense sadness and pain. I was reliving it all over again.

I talked to the social worker at the hospital about Joe. We talked about what he was like, different aspects of his personality. She was one person I spoke to who knew him, maybe at a different level than I knew him, but knew what I was talking about and saw what I saw and liked him. That was helpful, to feel that there were other people out there who really could understand what I saw and knew of him. It's different from talking to somebody who doesn't know this person from a hole in the head and can empathize with you, *may* know what it feels like, but didn't know Joe. . . .

QUESTIONING SELF-WORTH

I still have the suicide note. My friend says, "Give it back. Let it go, just let it go." I'm not really sure why I have it, except that it's addressed to me and that . . . I'm not ready to let it go. I could easily put it in his file, and I probably will when I'm ready.

Joe's father sent me a letter also. He had read all of Joe's journals and a lot of his writings. He saw a lot of despair. There were identity issues, sexuality issues, loneliness, real confusion. And his father had never really seen any of that from what Joe would articulate to his folks. His father never understood why Joe was so upset, because what he was presenting to his father didn't seem that important. It seemed like the kinds of issues we can all deal with and get by. He thought that he knew Joe the best, and he said he guessed he didn't. He thanked me and said I was one of many who tried to help Joe, and he wished people had been successful in their attempts. There was such pain in the letter. It must have been so hard to write. I didn't respond . . . What do you say? "Sorry" sounds so trite.

It's easier now to talk about it. I guess I came to grips—I hope I came to grips—[with the fact] that I couldn't change the outcome [but] that I do have something to offer to people, and with more experience, I can be good in my field. I want to be able to help people if I can and to make them feel, at least at the time that I'm with them, that they're important and that their feelings are important and that their pain is very real. . . .

Part of [my reaction to Joe's suicide] was just questioning my worth as this up-and-coming social worker. I always used to have the issue of separating the professional me from the personal me. How do I integrate the personal into the professional and know where to draw the lines? In the past, especially, there was more of a tendency for me to take people's problems home. I couldn't separate my work life from my personal and home life. That's one thing I did achieve over the past two years—I was able to separate them. But I couldn't just leave Joe's suicide at work. I used to ask people, "How do you deal with suicide? How do you work it through? How do I *process* this?"—a favorite word in social work classes—"I don't even know how to begin." So I just talked. Talk, talk, talk.

A Psychiatric Nurse Learns How to Cope with Her Brother's Suicide

by Karen Dunne-Maxim

Karen Dunne-Maxim has a degree in psychiatric nursing. She uses her training in managing the suicide prevention project of the Community of Mental Health Center in Piscataway, New Jersey. Through the project, she trains new counselors and talks to friends and family of suicide victims.

As Dunne-Maxim explains in the following selection, her advice to survivors comes not only from her medical training but also from her own experience as a survivor. While working as a public health nurse in the 1970s, Dunne-Maxim lost one of her brothers to suicide. His tragic death became a source of shame for Dunne-Maxim when she entered graduate school for psychiatric nursing. As Dunne-Maxim relates, only after sharing her secret with a supervisor was she able to confront the specter of her brother's death. The supervisor organized a meeting of graduate students who had also lost loved ones to suicide. From its humble beginnings, this group meeting transformed into an ongoing support program that drew in suicide survivors from throughout her community. Dunne-Maxim explains that only by talking through their confusion and resentment can those left behind find some solace.

Twenty years ago I lost my sixteen-year-old brother, Tim, to suicide. Tim was the youngest of seven children in my family. I was the oldest. He was editor of his yearbook, played the cello, and acted in a summer stock company with Olympia Dukakis. At the time of Tim's death, one of my brothers was a psychologist, another had a master's degree in guidance, and I was a public health nurse. In spite of our professional backgrounds, no one in our family recognized the signs of depression. Tim's depression was called a "masked depression," which means that the signs were not visible to other people. Looking back on it now, I can see that there were signs. He isolated himself from his close friends. He cut his stylish long hair into a crew cut.

WARNING SIGNS

One night Tim was picked up by the police because he was throwing stones at the headlights of cars. The police took him to a psychiatric hospital, where he was examined by a number of clinicians. He remained there overnight. My mother didn't know where he was until the following morning when the hospital called. She had been very worried because he had been acting strangely. For example, once when she was driving, he slammed his foot on the gas pedal. That was so out of character that she was shocked. When she asked the hospital staff if Tim was all right, the response was, "Yes. He told us he wanted to be in a psychiatric hospital because he was writing a novel about it." Curiously, that was something Tim would say. They discharged him that morning, Sunday morning. A very close friend of my mother's had died and she left Tim and went to the wake that afternoon. While she was away, my brother killed himself by jumping in front of a Long Island Rail Road train.

Even though Tim had been assessed by a number of professionals at the hospital, there was something about his illness that would not let him communicate with the very people who were trying to help him. How could this have happened? What was he thinking about? Tim's suicide made me realize that we have not done enough research into behavior patterns and biochemicals in the brain. (Biochemistry, referring to the chemistry of living organisms and its changes, is a fairly new branch of research. Levels of chemicals in the brain are measured to learn how they affect a person's mood.)

Tim's suicide cannot be explained as the result of a dysfunctional family. Although my father had a serious drinking problem, six members of the family became very productive members of society.

THE NEED TO TALK

After Tim died, I went to graduate school and studied psychiatric nursing. I didn't discuss the suicide with my colleagues because I thought that they would think less of me and less of my family. I even had a cousin working at my agency who thought that my brother died in a train accident. Tim's death became a family secret.

Then one day, one of my supervisors noticed that I was having trouble dealing with suicidal youngsters. I told her about Tim. My supervisor mentioned that three other students had lost family members to suicide and that none of them were talking about it publicly. She put us all together, and, along with my psychologist brother, we had our first meeting.

The meeting was very difficult. All of us survivors were therapists, yet it was very hard to talk about this subject. On the one hand, we were trained in the psychoanalytic mode that required us not to talk about ourselves. On the other hand, our training helped us to understand that we must come forward to overcome our feelings that the suicide was shameful, because it wasn't.

Our supervisor played a tape by a well-known family therapist, Norman Paul, who had done work on grief. He talked about researching his own family history in which he found out about a murder and a suicide. Hearing him talk in public about his family enabled us to confront our losses. What helped us the most was each other. We ended up forming a task force to review the literature on how families react to the aftermath of suicide. Then we held a conference for our professional colleagues where we identified ourselves as survivors. We knew that we had to step forward in order to help diminish the stigma.

CREATING A SUPPORT PROGRAM

Very soon thereafter we began meeting with three families for monthly educational and support groups. In nine and a half years I've worked with close to 800 surviving families.

At our meetings, a typical survivor's syndrome is the search for the *why*. It is something that is always there. Survivors get up every morning and search and search, but never find the answer. Some people had children or spouses with a mental illness. Even though they understood the ramifications of the illness, they wondered why the suicide occurred at that particular moment. Other suicides had shown no signs of mental illness at all.

At first survivors are in shock. They experience numbness. That is the body's way of letting the person take in the information slowly. There may be other physical reactions as well—the inability to eat or sleep, or butterflies in the stomach. That's all part of it. Gradually the symptoms lessen.

Often new members of the group express exaggerated feelings of responsibility for the death. Our family was no exception. We blamed ourselves for what we didn't do. My sister said, "If only I hadn't gone out that night." My brother returned from the Peace Corps and said, "If only I hadn't been so involved in my own life." And I said, "Gee, I should have told Tim to come out and live with me. Instead I said, 'You've been acting depressed, maybe you should talk to a counselor.'" Survivors look at what they didn't do. And these families are loving families.

Some survivors try to find the answer by blaming a scapegoat, but that's misplaced anger. They come up with simplistic explanations, such as, it was because his girlfriend broke up with him.

TALKING THROUGH THE PAIN

Because we don't know enough about depression, we are only able to view its patterns retrospectively. We realize now that my brother did things that were so out of character, such as cutting his long hair into a crew cut. Had he become psychotic at that point? We'll never know.

Some family members evade the blame by denial. Until the day he died, my father appeared to be convinced that Tim was in a train accident.

Survivors need help to get through the grief process. They can help themselves by learning about it and by talking about it. Talking is very important. Time helps, too. The pain lessens. Nevertheless, there will be many things that remind the survivors of the suicide. They may sometimes feel as though they are back to where they started, but they're really not.

It all comes down to the fact that if the person wanted to be saved, he or she would have told you, would have given a clear hint. But what suicides do instead is give out pieces of a puzzle. It is only after the death, when everybody's talking about it, that the friends and the family realize that they each got a piece of the puzzle.

Because there is little knowledge about the causes of suicide, to help prevent it we need to start by talking about it openly. Once people understand that suicide happens in the "nicest" families, much of the stigma will be taken away.

We're encouraging people to talk about suicide very openly. If there is a suicide in the family, we encourage the parents to tell their children about it right away, just like one does if a person dies of a heart attack.

A Psychiatrist Accepts Therapy for His Own Suicidal Feelings

by Kenneth F. Tullis

Kenneth F. Tullis is a psychiatrist with a private practice. He is a clinical assistant professor at the University of Tennessee Center for the Health Sciences, Department of Psychiatry in Memphis, Tennessee. He and his wife, Madge, have devoted their efforts to speaking about suicide prevention after Tullis was hospitalized for attempting to take his own life in 1982.

In the following selection, Tullis relates how childhood experiences filled him with intense fear. As he matured, Tullis recounts, his desire to succeed at school and his profession gave him some control of his world, but failures nagged at him and made his life seem worthless. He saw suicide as an option to end his pain and embarrassment.

While working as a hospital psychiatrist and contending with suicidal and traumatized patients, Tullis admits he became addicted to drugs and obsessed with suicide. When he tried to commit suicide in 1982 with an overdose of pills, he was rescued and resuscitated. Tullis was placed in a Houston, Texas, psychiatric facility for suicide therapy. There, Tullis admits, he felt awkward accepting help from his own colleagues, but in time he was able to overcome his suicidal feelings.

M y life was over. I knew that much.
January 1982, the neurotrauma unit. I came up from the depths, surfacing into a cold gray day. The IV hurt. The short backless hospital gown left my ass flapping in the breeze. My arms and legs were like overboiled pasta, flopping helplessly. Nurses came and went. I never looked up, never spoke. What was the point? Why should I do what everyone had always expected of me? I was dead.

And then the thoughts and feelings hit, slamming into me like breakers after a storm. I was *not* dead. I was full of fury at being alive. . . .

Everything *hurt*—life, in particular. If this was living, I wanted out, desperately.

I spent the next few days as a prisoner in Madison Heights, my own hospital [in Memphis]. The attendants, there around the clock, might wear white uniforms, but I knew better than that: they were guards. I hated them, too, dumb bastards. Some wanted to preach and pray over me; others pretended nothing had happened. Which was worse? I didn't know; I simply hated them all. . . .

SOMEONE BELIEVED IN ME

Unit secretary is a one-of-a-kind job on a psychiatric unit, about halfway between mother confessor and traffic controller, with a dash of cruise director. Robin was a good one. She cared about her work, but more importantly, she cared about her patients and their doctors—even me. As a doctor, I counted on her to route all the damn paperwork—charts, blood work, orders, consults. Robin would make it all happen, as though by magic.

I knew enough to believe in her, even if I could not believe in me. I trusted her, and I respected her opinion. She, of all people, could assess the psychiatrists like a Kennel Club judge at a dog show. If she thought well of me, that would carry some weight. And so, when the nurse's voice squawked through the white-box intercom strapped to my metal bed, "A 'Robin' to see you," something inside me yearned for her presence, as a prisoner on death row might want to see the chaplain.

She came slowly, softly, to the side of my bed. Her eyes were full of tears, and pain drew lines across her forehead. She took my hand, very gently, and looked into my eyes. I could not resist that quiet look. I felt full of shame and yet oddly safe. I had no words, no explanations, and she asked for none. No bullshit, no small talk, no social "I'm fine," because I wasn't fine and Robin and everyone else in the hospital knew it.

"Ken Tullis, I care about you," she said. Her voice was firm and compassionate, and I believed her—who knows why? "*We* care about you." I believed her again, without needing to know who "we" were. I'd been a practicing psychiatrist for seven years: I can judge tears, laughter, frowns, smiles, blankness, pain lines, you name it. Facial expressions and body language are my stock in trade. I knew she was for real. "Why don't you let us help you?" she whispered, her eyes brimming.

At that moment, something inside me unknotted, and warmth flowed back from my chest to my cold, hurting head. I felt my eyes grow moist and a tear rolled down the side of my face—a tear of peace. *My way almost got me killed, twice. My way got me back in this hospital two times, almost dead. What have I got to lose? Why not let them help?*

I rolled my wheelchair through the 8 Calvin psych unit door, the same door I had locked and unlocked for seven years, on my rounds to see my patients. The door clicked and locked behind me. I had no key. It didn't matter. I was home. . . .

A MOMENT OF CLARITY

Suicide was alive and well within me. Next time, I wouldn't fail.

I've never been a gun person; I preferred drug overdoses and hangings. But, now, guns looked promising. End of barrel in the mouth, reach for the trigger, blam! It's over. I had run this scenario through my head over and over in the past, always stopping short. I hadn't the guts to use the gun. Now I was finding the guts. No fear: just rage, raw and powerful. "Blow your head off," said the executioner, exultant and terrified. I hated who I had become.

God catches you in the strangest places . . . Three feet from the nurses' station, for example. I must have crossed that same spot thousands of times in the last seven years. Now I call it my God Spot. It wasn't a voice, merely something between a feeling and a thought. Sometimes the solution to a problem pops into your mind, effortlessly, after what seems like an endless struggle. It feels like the tumblers of a lock clicking into alignment and the lock opening. Something becomes possible that had not been possible before, however hard you'd worked at it. It was like that.

Two overdoses. Two best shots at suicide. I should be dead, but I'm not.

Abruptly I saw God, patiently and painfully watching me, staying with me, protecting me from each overdose. God just being present, not hating me, but suffering with me. God *wanting* my wellness and fullness of life, holding back, waiting for me to choose.

I didn't create myself. And I'm not in charge of when I die.

I kept it to myself at first, this knowledge, not sharing it with anyone. But in that single moment, something in me changed.

I left Memphis, heading for Houston and the Woodlawn Psychiatric Hospital, on January 24th. At the airport, I met the eyes of my three beautiful children, who were there to see me off. I had chosen, eighteen days before, to leave them by killing myself. Now, seeing them clearly, I felt a sudden pang of connection, a deep sadness for what I had put them through. I didn't want to leave them ever, but now I had to go, for their sakes and my own.

My wife, Madge, wasn't at the airport. She had done her bit to save me: now she was back in her childhood home, Shreveport. How could I blame her?

My father was with me on the flight to Houston. I had my last drink on the plane, a double gin martini. It felt like the last drink given a condemned man on his way to execution—and in fact it was. For a new man to have life, the old man had to die.

AT THE PSYCHIATRIC HOSPITAL

White House of Woodlawn Psychiatric Hospital was built in 1919. It sits out front, while behind it sprawl one-story red-brick buildings on grounds spotted with old trees. South Unit, the newest, is farthest back on the campus. Walking from White House to South Unit with a guard at my side took forever. All I could feel was fear: *Will I ever leave this place? Who's behind those locked doors? I don't know anyone here!*

I was on suicide watch. This time, I couldn't flee into the safe darkness. They'd left me no way to kill myself. I had to surrender all vestiges of my dignity—belt, keys, anything sharp. I ate with plastic utensils handed out, one meal at a time, by a tech stationed five feet from the dining table. And there was Nurse Rhoda, my very own daytime nightmare. She was one tough lady, and I hated her. I thought bitter and scandalous things about her, as I struggled down the hall holding my pants up with my hands.

At night, I couldn't sleep. I felt as though reality was closing in around me like a cloud of biting insects: I slapped them away, but they would not leave me in peace. I slipped into a sort of oblivion now and then, but spent what felt like eternity, night after night, staring into my own soul with a depth of self-loathing I cannot describe, until darkness closed over me.

And then it was morning, and morning was *hell*. Floods of awareness, and awareness meant reality, and reality sucked. I scanned my tiny room, looking for some exit, any way out of this; some rope of hope to hang myself with. Nothing. Suicide would have to wait.

Suicide watch ended, weeks later, with the ceremonial return of my belt. What a relief! Now at least I wouldn't have to hang onto my pants. I was actually grateful for something—a feeling I hadn't known for such a long time. And then I got real silverware, a metal knife and fork that didn't bend uselessly against every piece of mystery meat. "This is heaven!" I thought, cutting up my first meal as a free man. Heaven is a metal knife and fork. . . . Well, I was starting to learn.

ECHOES OF THE PAST

As life started to stir in me, I felt a wriggle of curiosity. Two questions terrified and yet intrigued me. I was afraid to ask them, and even more afraid to answer them, but they kept stirring irrepressibly: What went so terribly wrong in me? And how did a smart guy like me end up in a place like this?

My first memories are all fearful: hiding under the coffee table in terror and tears during a thunderstorm. Mom was away, and there was only the maid there with me. I think I knew then that the world is not a safe place. Going to Snowden School: now, *that* was *terror.* Such a small word for such a huge fear! First day of second grade: I dug in my heels and refused to leave the house. My father, wearing his big hat, walked me into my classroom to meet my new teacher. He left me there and walked out as I screamed—but silently, inside my own head—"Don't leave me!" Something deep inside me froze that day in 1950, and I've spent the rest of my life trying to find some way to thaw that frozen part out.

By grade four, I had started to find both my brain and my feet. I learned that my intelligence could set me free. Getting A's in my classes felt so good; they made my parents smile and earned my teacher's pleasure. Good grades could fill up the cold hole in the middle of me. They made the world safer. "As long as I can make A's, I'll be okay," I whispered to myself. But even so, there was a tiny niggle of doubt—a corner of insufficiency. Mom had told me when I was four that my father had been the smartest student ever in his medical school. Had he made even more A's? I wished she hadn't said that. . . .

By ninth grade, my shaky sense of confidence was just about stabilizing. I could think about the future. I had my course all charted: straight A's through school, med school just over the horizon. My sails were set and the waters ahead looked smooth and easy.

And then, just as the *Titanic* encountered its iceberg, so I encountered Mary Sims Dawson.

Grade 9 Latin. Latin scared me. Pop quizzes scared me. Even B's scared me. The possibility of an F sent cold terror down into my frozen gut. When I saw that big red F on the pop quiz in Latin, it meant not just "Failure," but "Fatal" and "Frozen" as well. There went my ship, torpedoed. So much for med school. So much for winning my parents' approval. So much for trust and confidence and hope.

I have to kill myself. The thought came from nowhere—or rather, it came from my own brain, the brain that had been going to set me free. Now that my brain had let me down, this thought came to rescue me. It consoled me. My sense of terror faded away; the trap opened, letting me go. I was free again. I had an option, a hope, a new course to set sail for, one that *I* controlled. It was a secret power, one I could hug to myself, and it killed the pain.

Randall College was my coming out, and Madge was my teacher. If I lacked confidence, she had it in abundance. An outgoing girl with a huge smile and a wonderful Shreveport southern drawl, Madge never met a stranger, only friends. For me, it was both love and jealousy at first sight. I hadn't a clue what to make of her. Could she thaw that frozen chunk deep inside me? Or would she rip all the sails of the ship I was sailing toward medical school? I didn't know which to fear more. . . .

BECOMING A PSYCHIATRIST

Finishing med school almost finished me. When Dean Caldwell called out, "Kenneth F. Tullis, M.D.!" a wave of terror hit me in the gut. I hated every possible medical specialty, eliminating each and every sort of internship and residency. I was adrift again, with no place to call home. For the first time, I realized that I didn't *want* to be a doctor. I'd got my M.D. only because my father had one.

Straight internal medicine internship was pure hell.

I took my first overdose later on in the summer of 1971—only twelve pills, but for me, a huge step forward. Neil Armstrong had nothing on me! This was a new option, a new fix. I was half scared to death and half exhilarated. Above all, I was *hooked.*

As for my profession, there was one specialty that I thought I could manage: psychiatry. "More teacher than doctor," I thought, remembering how fun and safe it felt to teach algerbra. "Besides, it might help fix me." This is a hell of a bad reason to become a shrink, but it's also surprisingly common. . . .

In my white coat, with the flowing color-coordinated label over the left breast pocket: Kenneth F. Tullis, M.D., I marched confidently through the halls of Madison Heights, making my rounds. I was . . . dedicated to sniffing out suicide and eradicating it from every floor of the hospital. With fifty pills inside me, no underwear (to ward off the heat rash caused by all those pills), suicide burning brightly at the back of my head, . . . I was the Hero Child. I would, by God, exterminate every symptom of emotional pain that crossed my path. . . .

Again and again in the years from '76 to '82, I would go into suicidal trances. Still in my white coat, I would go to 7 Calvin [a ward at the hospital], leave the elevator, turn first right and then left, slip through the back door into room 703, enter the biofeedback lab, slip the noose over my head, and try to kick the stool out from under my own feet. The hangman in me wrestled with the condemned prisoner in me, while the addict in me stood to one side and copped a magnificent high. Four times I came very close. Once, the hangman won, and I came out of my trance on the floor, the stool three feet away, and rope burns on my neck. For a moment, I was healthily terrified. But then the flame steadied and leapt high again.

From then on, I was in a losing battle with my god and lover, Death. Suicide stayed with me every waking moment, at home, at work, on break, whenever. It was only a matter of time.

Wednesday, January 6, 1982. In my own office, Calvin 703, I reached into the top left-hand drawer of my desk. Days before, during rounds, I had found and confiscated a bottle of Dilantin, and phenobarbital from one of my patients, an impulsive young man on 8 Calvin. I had a bottle of booze in my desk as well. I took the two together, read my Bible for awhile, and waited to walk straight into my lover's arms.

OFF SUICIDE WATCH

So there I was in the winter of '82, off suicide watch at Woodlawn, in Houston, Texas, feeling absurdly grateful for metal cutlery and my belt. Off suicide watch meant off South Unit, and off South Unit meant starting my classes. Off to school again. Some things never change. This time, I had no mom, no dad, no Madge: only a guard— but a friendly guard. I felt childishly happy to have a friend to walk with me to school. I felt . . . safe.

"*No grades! This school has no grades! I can't make an F!*" I shouted to myself. All I had to do was suit up and show up and I'd be okay. It was a wonderful gift, a blessing. A *uniform—I need a uniform*. I chose my blue tennis warmups—*with* underwear, now that I didn't have to worry about heat rash from those fifty pills. Art therapy had taught me that blue was my safe color. And the pants' drawstring waist let me keep my precious belt safe in my own room. . . .

Woodlawn was a "do it, don't think it, enjoy it, don't analyze it" sort of place. The kid in me loved it. The adult side of me hated it and wanted out *now*. In this internal war I was, for the first time, siding with the kid.

Something was also starting to draw me to chapel on Sunday mornings—I didn't know why I couldn't understand what the attraction was. Few other patients came, but still, I kept on going. Was it some old church tape, something bouncing around in my unconscious from childhood? I'd grown up in a church where Sunday morning means Sunday school: that fact had been etched into my mind. Now that the drugs were out of my system, the etching was still there. So I sat in the chapel, obedient as a trained dog, long after the bell had rung. . . .

I'd always seen God as sitting above me in judgment, looking over his glasses in scorn, waiting to take potshots and find fault with everything I did and was. I imagined God raining F's down on me whatever I did, however hard I tried. I saw God as setting up a standard that I could not possibly meet, and judging me against that standard, without kindness or mercy. Now I found a new God, a friend, companionably beside me. And I knew he had been there all along, waiting for me: patient, silent, constant—with faith in me, as I had never had faith in him. . . .

IN THERAPY

May 1982, Madge was pissed, *really* pissed. I didn't think that was fair. After all, I wrote at least once a week, even when I didn't want to. . . . I still fantasized about shedding wife and kids and setting up a bachelor pad with megawatts of stereo equipment. . . .

Kevin Johnson—Dr. Bushy-Brows—. . . meant *business*—no B.S. allowed! Worse still, he'd treated my father. *I've got my dad's shrink.* I screamed into my pillow, the night before my therapy began.

Kevin didn't appreciate my plan for the bachelor pad. That pissed me off. He wanted to "explore it." Explore it! I wanted to *do* it. *Don't throw this therapy shit at me, doc!* But I locked my anger away, keeping it safe from being seen—or healed. It took me five months to get up enough nerve to admit to him that I was angry at him.

He could use those bushy eyebrows like a marksman uses a rifle. "You know," he said, raising one of them, "I'm not sure you're capable of commitment.". . . .

Eyebrow #2: ready, aim, fire: "You never really made a commitment to your marriage or to Madge." Direct hit. He was right, dead right, and the knowledge stunned me. . . .

Madge came to visit—our first therapeutic visit. We had four hours together, with a guard close by. Within five minutes, we were raging at each other on the tennis court. She almost left me there. *Don't you know who I am?* But I feared that maybe she did know. That same struggle between wanting to be understood and not wanting to be seen with any clarity at all. . . . We came so close that day to breaking our marriage. My life fell apart a little bit more.

On the other hand, life in the puzzle factory was definitely improving. I was starting to gain confidence, starting to feel better. My teachers seemed happy with me. Freud would have been pretty pleased, I imagined. So I was happy with me, too. In therapy with Bushy-Brows one day, I was spouting off cheap insight with great enthusiasm, showing off my Woodlawn-Patient-of-the-Year persona, when he trained his eyebrows on me, sighting for bear again.

"And tell me, Ken: do you plan to do something about your drug addiction before you go back to Memphis?"

Nice technique, I thought approvingly. *At least 9.5. Drug addiction? Me?* I cast my mind back over my time at Woodlawn. Not once had I craved a drug, not even once. *Wrong man. Not me!*

Leaning forward in his chair, eyebrows up, Bushy-Brows moved in closer. "I want you to contact the Impaired Physicians Program here in Houston," he said, looking me straight in the eyes. At once my heart went out to those poor impaired physicians, whom I was clearly called upon to help. They *needed* me. How could I possibly refuse?

IMPAIRED PHYSICIANS PROGRAM

In Lynn's car, on my way to my first meeting, I was on pins and needles, waiting to meet the poor doc whom I'd help that night. As we drove, Lynn told me his story—the depressions, the drugs, the divorce, the shock treatments, the agony. Then he leaned toward me, asking in that "I know something you don't know" voice: "Do you know what was wrong with me?"

"No, what?" I said.

"I'm an addict!" he proclaimed.

"No way!" I thought, amazed. "I'm one, too!" At that moment, years of denial melted away like snow under strong sun. *I* was the poor doc who got helped that night. I'd come home.

Paul strolled up to me after that first meeting, a big smile on his face, and thrust out his hand. "Woodlawn," he said with a sort of questioning authority. "Two years ago."

"Yep," I answered, much as I'd announce my alma mater.

"What unit?" he asked.

"South."

"Me, too. What doc?"

"Johnson."

"Me, too. What room?"

"Last one on the left."

"Me, too."

This was giving me goose bumps. I felt as though God had sent me my very own angel that evening. . . .

Dr. Bushy-Brows was starting to make more sense. Affirming the changes in me, he encouraged me to stick with Paul and the doctors' group. I was starting to *like* my therapist. The first time I cried with him, it felt so safe—a warm, fuzzy feeling I'd never experienced before.

Madge and I, meanwhile, took the best step we'd taken in years: we put our marriage on a one-day-at-a-time standing. What freedom! We gave each other the freedom to stay or go each morning. We chose, that first morning, to stay, both of us, and we have made the same choice every morning since.

As denial melted away, each stretch of truth became clearer. I realized that I'd been addicted not just to drugs, but to women, too: for me, mood-altering sex was exactly like mood-altering pills. If I fell back into those two traps, I'd end up killing myself. And then there was work. . . . I realized, sadly, that working at Madison Heights would threaten my sobriety. It was too big a risk. Madge, our son Ken, and my dad—bless them—struggled to dismantle my old office. But with Calvin 703 gone, would I ever be able to work again?

August 10, 1982. It was a long, long struggle, but I faced the reality: it was time to go back out into the world. All I could do was to trust in God to carry me through. "If you think I need another year here on South, I'll do it," I told Dr. Munford on rounds that day, meaning every word of it. He paused, looking at me thoughtfully, and said, "We've set your discharge date. September 10." My heart almost stopped.

Saying good-bye to Woodlawn was almost as painful and terrifying as stepping through those doors and onto suicide watch nine months before. The "I don't want to go!" part of me screamed inside my head, as I'd screamed to stay home from second grade, years ago. But another part of me knew that I had to go, just as I'd had to leave my kids at the airport back in January. To grow, I had to let go and move on.

My final good-bye was to Dr. Munford, who had been my doctor and attending psychiatrist. A G.P.-turned-psychiatrist, he brought common sense, firmness, and great wisdom to his work. I had come to trust and love him deeply, hoping some day to become more the man he was. "Ken," he said in our last moments together, "you will always have us with you.". . .

"I do have one concern for you that I want to share," he went on. I nodded, too close to tears to speak. "I don't think you're finished with your struggle with suicide."

Terror hit me. "*No!*" I screamed inside my head. The flame had been out for months: now it was awake again. Or had it ever really gone out? Driving away from Woodlawn with Madge, I realized that it had been there all along, but burning so low I hadn't noticed it. I'd been distracted, too preoccupied with the Twelve Steps [recovery program] and other new and healthy things to pay it any attention. But every mile we drove left the flame a little stronger. By the time we got to Memphis, it was burning bright and strong.

AMERICAN ASSOCIATION OF SUICIDOLOGY (AAS)

5221 Wisconsin Ave. NW, Washington, DC 20015
(202) 237-2280 • fax: (202) 237-2282
e-mail: info@suicidology.org • Web site: www.suicidology.org

The AAS is one of the largest suicide prevention organizations in the United States. It promotes the view that suicidal thoughts are almost always a symptom of depression and that suicide is almost never a rational decision. In addition to prevention of suicide, the group also works to increase public awareness about suicide and to help those grieving the death of a loved one to suicide. The association publishes the quarterly newsletters *American Association of Suicidology—Newslink* and *Surviving Suicide* and the quarterly journal *Suicide and Life Threatening Behavior.*

AMERICAN FOUNDATION FOR SUICIDE PREVENTION (AFSP)

120 Wall St., 22nd Fl., New York, NY 10005
(888) 333-AFSP • fax: (212) 363-6237
e-mail: inquiry@afsp.org • Web site: www.afsp.org

Formerly known as the American Suicide Foundation, the AFSP supports scientific research on depression and suicide, educates the public and professionals on the recognition and treatment of depressed and suicidal individuals, and provides support programs for those coping with the loss of a loved one to suicide. It opposes the legalization of physician-assisted suicide. The AFSP publishes a policy statement on physician-assisted suicide, the newsletter *Crisis*, and the quarterly *Lifesavers.*

AMERICAN LIFE LEAGUE (ALL)

PO Box 1350, Stafford, VA 22555
(540) 659-4171 • fax: (540) 659-2586
e-mail: whylife@all.org • Web site: www.all.org

The league believes that human life is sacred. It works to educate Americans about the dangers of all forms of euthanasia and opposes legislative efforts that would legalize or increase its incidence. ALL publishes the bimonthly pro-life magazine *Celebrate Life* and distributes videos, brochures, and newsletters monitoring euthanasia-related developments.

AMERICAN PSYCHIATRIC ASSOCIATION (APA)

1000 Wilson Blvd., Suite 1825, Arlington, VA 22209-3901
(703) 907-7300
e-mail: apa@psych.org • Web site: www.psych.org

An organization of psychiatrists dedicated to studying the nature, treatment, and prevention of mental disorders, the APA helps create mental health policies, distributes information about psychiatry, and promotes psychiatric research and education. It publishes the *American Journal of Psychiatry* and *Psychiatric News* monthly.

AMERICAN PSYCHOLOGICAL ASSOCIATION

750 First St. NE, Washington, DC 20002-4242
(800) 374-2721 • fax: (202) 336-5500
e-mail: public.affairs@apa.org • Web site: www.apa.org

This professional organization for psychologists aims to "advance psychology as a science, as a profession, and as a means of promoting human welfare." It produces numerous publications, including the book *Adolescent Suicide: Assessment and Intervention*, the report "Researcher Links Perfectionism in High Achievers with Depression and Suicide," and the online guide *Warning Signs—a Violence Prevention Guide for Youth.*

CANADIAN ASSOCIATION FOR SUICIDE PREVENTION (CASP)

c/o the Support Network
301–11456 Jasper Ave. NW, Edmonton, AB T5K 0M1 Canada
(780) 482-0198 • fax: (780) 488-1495
e-mail: casp@suicideprevention.ca
Web site: www.thesupportnetwork.com/CASP/library.html

CASP organizes annual conferences and educational programs on suicide prevention. It publishes the newsletter *CASP News* three times a year and the booklet *Suicide Prevention in Canadian Schools.*

CENTRE FOR SUICIDE PREVENTION

1202 Centre St. SE, Suite 320, Calgary, AB T2G 5A5 Canada
(403) 245-3900 • fax: (403) 245-0299
e-mail: csp@suicideinfo.ca • Web site: www.suicideinfo.ca

The centre acquires and distributes information on suicide prevention. It maintains a computerized database, a free mailing list, and a document delivery service. It is also linked to the Suicide Information Education Collection, a library and resource center on suicide and suicide prevention.

COMPASSION & CHOICES

PO Box 101810, Denver, CO 80250-1810
(800) 247-7421 • fax: (303) 639-1224
e-mail: info@compassionandchoices.org
Web site: www.compassionandchoices.org

Compassion & Choices (formerly the Hemlock Society) believes that terminally ill individuals have the right to commit suicide. The society publishes books on suicide, death, and dying, including *Final Exit*, a guide for those suffering with terminal illnesses and considering suicide. The organization also publishes *Compassion & Choices* magazine.

DEPRESSION AND BIPOLAR SUPPORT ALLIANCE

730 N. Franklin St., Suite 501, Chicago, IL 60610-7204
(800) 826-3632 • (312) 642-0049 • fax: (312) 642-7243
e-mail: questions@dbsalliance.org • Web site: www.dbsalliance.org

The alliance provides support and advocacy for patients with depression and manic-depressive illness. It seeks to persuade the public that these disorders are biochemical in nature and to end the stigmatization of people who suffer from them. It publishes various books and pamphlets, some of which can be downloaded for free from its Web site.

DEPRESSION AND RELATED AFFECTIVE DISORDERS ASSOCIATION (DRADA)

2330 W. Joppa Rd., Suite 100, Lutherville, MD 21093
(410) 583-2919
e-mail: drada@jhmi.edu • Web site: www.drada.org

DRADA, a nonprofit organization that works in cooperation with the Department of Psychiatry at the Johns Hopkins University School of Medicine, seeks to alleviate the suffering arising from depression and manic depression by assisting self-help groups, providing education and information, and lending support to research programs. It publishes the report "A Look at . . . Suicide, a Relentless and Underrated Foe" and the book *Night Falls Fast: Understanding Suicide.*

NATIONAL ALLIANCE FOR THE MENTALLY ILL (NAMI)

Colonial Place Three, 2107 Wilson Blvd., Suite 300, Arlington, VA 22201
(703) 524-7600 • fax: (703) 524-9094
Web site: www.nami.org

NAMI is a consumer advocacy and support organization composed largely of family members of people with severe mental illnesses such as schizophrenia, manic-depressive illness, and depression. The alliance adheres to the position that severe mental illnesses are biological brain diseases and that mentally ill people should not be blamed or stigmatized for their conditions. NAMI favors increased government funding for research, treatment, and community services for the mentally ill. Its publications include the bimonthly newsletter *NAMI Advocate* well as various brochures, handbooks, and policy recommendations.

NATIONAL FOUNDATION FOR DEPRESSIVE ILLNESS (NAFDI)

PO Box 2257, New York, NY 10116
(800) 239-1265
Web site: www.depression.org

NAFDI informs the public, health care providers, and corporations about depression and manic-depressive illness. It promotes the view that these disorders are physical illnesses treatable with medication, and it believes that such medication should be made readily available to those who need it. The foundation maintains several toll-free telephone lines and distributes brochures, bibliographies, and literature on the symptoms of and treatments for depression and manic-depressive illness. It also publishes the quarterly newsletter *NAFDI News.*

SAMARITANS

10 The Grove, Slough, Berkshire SL1 1QP UK
08457 90 90 90 UK
e-mail: jo@samaritans.org • Web site: www.samaritans.org.uk

Samaritans is the largest suicide prevention organization in the world. Established in England in 1953, the organization now has branches in at least forty-four nations throughout the world. The group's volunteers provide counseling and other assistance to suicidal and despondent individuals. In addition, Samaritans publishes the booklets *Elderly Suicide, Teen Suicide Information and Guidelines for Parents,* and *The Suicidal Student: A Guide for Educators.*

SUICIDE AWARENESS\VOICES OF EDUCATION (SA\VE)

9001 E. Bloomington Fwy., Suite 150, Bloomington, MN 55420
(952) 946-7998
Web site: www.save.org

SA\VE works to prevent suicide and to help those grieving after the suicide of a loved one. Its members believe that brain diseases, such as depression, should be detected and treated promptly because they can result in suicide. In addition to pamphlets and the book *Suicide: Survivors—a Guide for Those Left Behind,* the organization publishes the quarterly newsletter *Voices.*

SUICIDE PREVENTION ACTION NETWORK USA (SPAN USA)

1025 Vermont Ave. NW, Suite 1200, Washington, DC 20005
(202) 449-3600 • fax: (202) 449-3601
e-mail: info@spanusa.org • Web site: www.spanusa.org

The Suicide Prevention Action Network is dedicated to combating suicide by increasing public awareness, instigating community action, and advocating federal, state, and local grassroots policy making Its members include people who have survived a loved one's suicide, suicide attempters and those with suicidal thoughts, professionals who provide care to families and communities, community leaders, and concerned citizens. SPAN USA boasts among its accomplishments the passage of several successful laws to aid in the struggle for suicide prevention, helping to draft the National Strategy for Suicide Prevention, and cofounding the National Council for Suicide Prevention.

SUICIDE PREVENTION RESOURCE CENTER (SPRC)

Education Development Center, 55 Chapel St., Newton, MA 02458-1060
877-GET-SPRC (438-7772)
e-mail: info@sprc.org • Web site: www.sprc.org

The Suicide Prevention Resource Center works in conjunction with several partner organizations, including the American Association of Suicidology and the American Foundation for Suicide Prevention, to provide the necessary expertise and resources for training practices in suicide prevention. The SPRC offers various online means through which professionals can learn about current methods of suicide prevention as well as prevention support, training, conferences and Web-based resources.

YELLOW RIBBON INTERNATIONAL SUICIDE PREVENTION PROGRAM

PO Box 644, Westminster, CO 80036-0644
(303) 429-3530 • fax: (303) 426-4496
e-mail: ask4help@yellowribbon.org • Web site: www.yellowribbon.org

The Yellow Ribbon Suicide Prevention Program is a comprehensive educational strategy to help teens and others afflicted with depression or suicidal behavior to seek help for their problems. The organization sponsors suicide awareness events nationwide and provides resources for suicide prevention training. Chapters of the Yellow Ribbon International Suicide Prevention Program may be found in nearly every state in the United States as well as in Europe.

BOOKS

Jean Amery, *On Suicide: A Discourse on Voluntary Death.* Trans. John D. Barlow. Bloomington: Indiana University Press, 1999.

G. Lloyd Carr, *Fierce Goodbye: Living in the Shadow of Suicide.* Scottsdale, PA: Herald, 2004.

Sue Chance, *Stronger than Death: When Suicide Touches Your Life.* New York: Norton, 1992.

George Howe Colt, *The Enigma of Suicide: A Timely Investigation into the Causes, the Possibilities for Prevention, and the Paths to Healing.* New York: Simon & Schuster, 1992.

John Donelly, *Suicide: Right or Wrong?* Amherst, NY: Prometheus, 1998.

Joan Esherick, *The Silent Cry: A Teen's Guide to Escaping Self-Injury and Suicide.* Broomall, PA: Mason Crest, 2004.

Louis Everstine, *The Anatomy of Suicide: Silence of the Heart.* Springfield, IL: Charles C. Thomas, 1998.

Sara K. Goldsmith, *Reducing Suicide: A National Imperative.* Washington, DC: National Academies Press, 2002.

Earl A. Grollman, *Living When a Young Friend Commits Suicide: Or Even Starts Talking About It.* Boston: Beacon, 1999.

Herbert Hendin, *Suicide in America.* New York: W.W. Norton, 1996.

Kay Redfield Jamison, *Night Falls Fast: Understanding Suicide.* New York: Vintage, 2000.

Robert A. King, Alan Apter, and Ian M. Goodyer, *Suicide in Children and Adolescents.* Cambridge, NY: Cambridge University Press, 2003.

Antoon A. Leenaars, *Suicide Notes: Predictive Clues and Patterns.* New York: Human Sciences, 1988.

David Lester, *The Cruelest Death: The Enigma of Adolescent Suicide.* Philadelphia: Charles, 1992.

————, *Making Sense of Suicide: An In-depth Look at Why People Kill Themselves.* Philadelphia: Charles, 1997.

David Lester and Margot Tallmer, *Now I Lay Me Down: Suicide in the Elderly.* Philadelphia: Charles, 1993.

Christopher Lukas and Henry M. Seiden, *Silent Grief: Living in the Wake of Suicide.* Northvale, NJ: Jason Aronson, 1997.

Alvin F. Poussaint, *Lay My Burden Down: Suicide and the Mental Health Crisis Among African-Americans.* Boston: Beacon, 2001.

Paula M. Quinn, *Shadow on My Soul: Overcoming Addiction to Suicide.* Manchester, CT: Knowledge, Ideas & Trends, 1995.

Ralph Rickgarn, *Perspectives on College Student Suicide: Death, Value, and Meaning.* Amityville, NY: Baywood, 1994.

William A. Ritter, *Take the Dimness of My Soul Away: Healing After a Loved One's Suicide.* Harrisburg, PA: Morehouse, 2004.

Edwin S. Schneidman, *Comprehending Suicide: Landmarks in 20th-Century Suicidology.* Washington, DC: American Psychological Association, 2001.

Mark Seinfelt, *Final Drafts: Suicides of World-Famous Authors.* Amherst, NY: Prometheus, 1999.

Geo Stone, *Suicide and Attempted Suicide: Methods and Consequences.* New York: Carroll & Graf, 2001.

Kevin Taylor, *Seduction of Suicide: Understanding and Recovering from an Addiction to Suicide.* Bloomington, IN: Authorhouse, 2002.

Robert I. Yufit and David Lester, *Coping with Suicide: Assessment, Treatment, and Prevention of Suicidal Behavior.* Hoboken, NJ: John Wiley, 2004.

PERIODICALS

Katja Becker and Martin H. Schmidt, "When Kids Seek Help On-line: Internet Chat Rooms and Suicide," *Reclaiming Children and Youth,* Winter 2005.

Albert C. Cain, "Children of Suicide: The Telling and the Knowing,"

Psychiatry: Interpersonal and Biological Processes, Summer 2002.

Silvia Sara Canetto and David Lester, "Love and Achievement Motives in Women's and Men's Suicide Notes," *Journal of Psychology*, September 2002.

K.R. Conner, A.L. Beautrais, and Y. Conwell, "Researchers Find a Relationship Between Alcohol Dependence, Mood Disorders, and Suicide," *DATA: The Brown University Digest of Addiction Theory & Application*, December 2003.

Diego De Leo, "Culture and Suicide in Late Life," *Psychiatric Times*, October 15, 2003.

Elizabeth Fried Ellen, "Suicide Prevention on Campus," *Psychiatric Times*, October 1, 2002.

Elizabeth F. Farrell, "A Suicide and Its Aftermath," *Chronicle of Higher Education*, May 24, 2002.

Max Fink, "Suicide Risk Reduced," *Psychiatric Times*, February 1, 2005.

Deeanna Franklin, "Education Key to Suicide Prevention on Campus," *Clinical Psychiatry News*, October 2004.

————, "Most Suicides Take Place During Spring, Not Winter Holidays," *Family Practice News*, April 15, 2004.

Keith Hawton and Kathryn Williams, "Influences of the Media on Suicide," *British Medical Journal*, December 14, 2002.

Bernadine Healy, "Dying of Depression: Psychology of Teenagers and Teenage Suicide," *U.S. News & World Report*, November 10, 2003.

Susan Horsburgh, "Cause of Death, Suicide, Age 8: Angelica Gutierrez's Self-Inflicted Death in the Third Grade Raises a Disturbing Question—Why Are More Preteens Taking Their Own Lives?" *People Weekly*, September 15, 2003.

Debra Houry, "Suicidal Patients in the Emergency Department: Who Is at the Greatest Risk?"*Annals of Emergency Medicine*, June 2004.

Jerry Ingram, "Understudied Groups Need Targeted Suicide Prevention," *Clinical Psychiatry News*, May 2004.

Rachel Jenkins, "Addressing Suicide as a Public-Health Problem," *Lancet*, March 9, 2002.

Ruth Grant Kalischuk and Virginia E. Hayes, "Grieving, Mourning, and Healing Following Youth Suicide: A Focus on Health and Well Being in Families," *Omega: Journal of Death & Dying*, 2003–2004.

Jeremy Kisch, E. Victor Leino, and Morton M. Silverman, "Aspects of Suicidal Behavior, Depression, and Treatment in College Students," *Suicide and Life-Threatening Behavior*, February 2005.

Mental Health Weekly, "Children Whose Parents Attempt Suicide Are at High Risk for Attempting Suicide," September 16, 2002.

Robert Pool, "The Why of It All: By Their Own Hands, More than 30,000 Americans Die Every Year," *Florida Trend*, February 2004.

A. Preti, "Unemployment and Suicide: How Is Your Work Going?" *Journal of Epidemiology & Community Health*, August 2003.

Julie Scelfo, "Preventing Suicides," *Newsweek*, November 3, 2003.

Carl Sherman, "Common Themes Are Found in Cases Involving Suicide," *Clinical Psychiatry News*, March 2003.

Gunjan Sinha, "Child Suicide, by the Numbers," *Popular Science*, September 2002.

Howard N. Snyder, "Is Suicide More Common Inside or Outside of Juvenile Facilities?" *Corrections Today*, February 2005.

Justice Staff, "Assessing American Indian Suicide Risk: Can Screening Be Culturally Sensitive?" *Corrections Today*, June 2004.

Elaine Adams Thompson et al., "The Mediating Roles of Anxiety, Depression, and Hopelessness on Adolescent Suicidal Behaviors," *Suicide and Life-Threatening Behavior*, February 2005.

Erica Weir, "Suicide: The Hidden Epidemic," *Canadian Medical Association Journal*, September 4, 2001.

Leigh A. Willis et al., "Uncovering the Mystery: Factors of African American Suicide," *Suicide and Life-Threatening Behavior*, Winter 2003.

Women in Higher Education, "Saving Student Lives with Healthy Campuses," November 2004.